# Carriers of Faith

# Carriers of Faith

## Lessons from Congregational Studies

A festschrift
in honor of Robert W. Lynn

### Edited by
## Carl S. Dudley
## Jackson W. Carroll
## James P. Wind

Westminster/John Knox Press
Louisville, Kentucky

*Book design by Ken Taylor*

*First edition*

Published by Westminster/John Knox Press
Louisville, Kentucky

PRINTED IN THE UNITED STATES OF AMERICA
9 8 7 6 5 4 3 2 1

**Library of Congress Cataloging-in-Publication Data**

Carriers of faith : lessons from congregational studies / edited by
Carl S. Dudley, Jackson W. Carroll, James P. Wind. — 1st ed.
     p.    cm.
"A festschrift in honor of Robert W. Lynn."
Includes bibliographical references.
ISBN 0-664-25204-4

  1. Pastoral theology.  2. Parishes.  I. Dudley, Carl S., 1932–    .
II. Carroll, Jackson W.  III. Wind, James P., 1948–    .
IV. Lynn, Robert W.
BV4011.C312   1990
250—dc20                           90-38425

# Dedication 〉〈←

Robert Wood Lynn's career has stretched thus far from his early years in Wheatland, Wyoming, to retirement in Leeds, Maine. During the first sixty-five years of his still unfolding journey, he has completed programs of study at Princeton University, Yale Divinity School, and Union Theological Seminary, has served in the United States Army and in the ministry of the Presbyterian Church, has taught practical theology, religion, and education at Union Theological Seminary in New York and, as vice-president of the Lilly Endowment, Inc., has directed the largest program of grant-making in the field of religious inquiry in America.

Dr. Lynn has helped revitalize religious communities throughout America, shaping and supporting numerous research projects and serving as consultant to both institutions and individuals. He is known as foremost among students of the history of theological education in America, and has written many articles and books in the field. His legacy is found in the careers of many scholars and in the mission of many congregations, communities, seminaries, and universities. His special concerns have brought together black and white, Protestant, Catholic, and Jew, providing them opportunities to understand and learn from each other, to strengthen America's religious institutions, and to increase the quality of our nation's religious and intellectual life. Together with his wife, Katharine, and their children, Thomas, Janet, Elizabeth, and Sarah, Robert Lynn has created a warm environment of teaching and learning that many have found nurturing and life-affecting.

The authors of this book have received Dr. Lynn's encouragement to understand and improve congregational life. This aspect of American religion was neglected until he urged researchers to pay attention to the congregations in which the faith and morals of millions of believers are formed and transformed.

To honor Robert Lynn's conviction that congregations are the place where theory meets practice, we offer insights from our research, which we think will help pastors and lay persons become more effective leaders.

# Contents ✳←

# Introduction  ✳←

Not too long ago it was fashionable to predict the demise of the congregation as an effective religious institution and to call for some sort of new entity that could surpass it. Now styles are changing and a new view of congregations is emerging—one that seeks to take these institutions seriously, to understand them, to contribute to their future life. While not yet a universal viewpoint in our society, this perspective has drawn more and more people to reconsider these institutions. So many, in fact, that we now have this book written by people who are devoting their energies to such reconsideration and reappraisal. Something new is going on.

From various denominational, professional, and personal backgrounds, these authors have been drawn into the orbit of congregational studies. Something about these institutions has captured their interest. For various reasons they cannot let go of congregations. Their interests range from the basic human quest for community to grand theological searches for the sacred. They approach these institutions from various starting points: Protestant, Catholic, black, white, male, female, academic, practitioner. Despite their differences, each of these authors shares a basic fascination, an elemental curiosity, about a form of religious life that is as close as the neighborhood filling station yet can seem as exotic as the most distant tribal village.

Why this fascination with the congregation? Perhaps it is because our so-called secular society has more than 346,000 of them. Or because on any given weekend 40 percent of postmodern Americans, despite all the options available to them, will be found within their precincts. We give almost $12 billion a year to them. Membership statistics, in spite of occasional dips, have increased over the last century from 41 million to more than 142 million. The size of the congregational phenomenon in our society, especially when considered alongside indicators from other countries,

9

may be reason enough to lure some to take a second look at congregations. Something is going on here.

Many of these authors have also puzzled over the sheer tenacity of these institutions. Why, when their neighborhoods change, their buildings decay, their leaders falter, or their hopes fizzle, do congregations keep on going? Sometimes the biggest mystery of all is that so many of them survive and even flourish. Periodically, reformers have arisen in the American context: the itinerants of the Great Awakenings, the revivalists of the evangelical movement, the leaders of the institutional church movement and the social gospelers of the late nineteenth and early twentieth centuries, the missionary-structures advocates of the 1950s and 1960s, the televangelists of the 1970s and 1980s, and the host of parachurch organizers who create cells, special interest groups, or alternative communities. The reformers have not had to look far to find fault with America's congregations. And they always offered some kind of more-than-congregational alternative. Yet congregations remain, long after the reformers have failed, succeeded, or moved on to other causes.

But most of these congregations do much more than survive. They make a difference. For good and ill, these institutions intervene in people's daily lives. They are places where life's passages are celebrated and mourned. They are repositories of meaning and laboratories where people try out and try on moral stances. These are the institutions where the voluntary spirit is nurtured and, occasionally, dashed. These are places that can be communities of great care or caverns of cold unconcern. In these places people find and express values they can share or oppose, causes they can support or resist, groups they can join or ignore. In this congregational zone a bridge is often built between life's private and public spheres—allowing people to connect deep personal beliefs with large public matters. And in this zone people are also often lured into thinking that God is present with special concern for a chosen few. Because congregations make a difference, people—members, pastors, and now scholars who specialize in congregational studies—find themselves drawn to them.

The most amazing thing about these ordinary institutions is that people come to them for an encounter with the extraordinary. That we still seek such encounters—with God, grace, the uncanny—is no small wonder. That we seek such encounters here, more than anywhere else, is a bit more to ponder. Personal searches for ultimate meaning, for hope, for salvation often begin and come to focus at fonts, around altars, beneath pulpits, in pews. The sacred leaves its traces here and people return for fresh sightings, scents, tastes, sounds, and renewal of the spirit.

What should readers look for on these pages? Certainly a diversity of congregational experiences and methods will manifest themselves here. The chapters that follow allow readers to enter a variety of scholarly and professional workshops where various techniques and skills are brought to bear on the congregation. As they look over the shoulders of these different workers, some of whom are laboring to understand, others striving to change, and others seeking to do both, readers will have opportunity to consider new approaches to their own situations. Here is a safe place to be challenged to try out some new possibilities.

But readers should also be alert to the ways in which these essays hover around a common theme: congregations as carriers of faith. In its early chapters this book seeks to identify and understand key dimensions in the complex process of modern transmission of faith. Then the book goes on to consider strategies for enhancing, directing, and changing that process. Together these authors are experimenting with new ways to look at congregations—as carriers or bearers of traditions, languages, symbol systems, worldviews, and action styles. If they open new angles of vision for those who do not know congregations very well and especially for those who know them best, then the lessons learned in congregational studies may enrich congregational life in ways we have not yet anticipated.

James P. Wind

# PART ONE

# Perspectives

# ONE

# Memory, Amnesia, and History

## JAMES P. WIND AND JAMES W. LEWIS

American congregations live and perhaps have always lived in paradoxical circumstances. They are simultaneously places of memory and places of amnesia. On the one hand, they bear traditions—legacies of once (still?) powerful pasts. On the other, they manifest the quintessential American penchant for freedom from constraints of the past and openness to new possibilities of the present and future. Those who belong to congregations inevitably find themselves squeezed between two contrary impulses—tradition's pressure to remember and modernity's pressure to forget. This tension is one source of the amazing creativity attested to by the variety of congregational forms and styles found on the American landscape. It is also a primary factor in many congregational pathologies; a source of breakdown, conflict, and entropy.

In this chapter we wish to describe this common congregational dilemma. To do so we will first discuss the two sides of a congregation's historical character, its traditional and its American face. Having identified the dual personality structure shared by all American congregations, we will then illustrate by way of a case study the consequences of such a tension in actual congregational life. We will conclude the chapter by suggesting how historical perspective can contribute to fresh understandings of congregational experience. Unearthing a congregation's history cannot remove this fundamental tension felt by any American church, parish, or synagogue. But it can contribute to an understanding of the tension and the formation of an intentional approach toward this frequently overlooked feature of congregational life.

## Places of Memory

In his book *Treasure in Earthen Vessels*, James M. Gustafson (1985:73) claimed that "common memory makes possible common life." If our churches are anything more than mere aggregates of self-actualizing individuals, it is because shared memories make possible shared understandings and perceptions. What Michael Goldberg (1985:13) calls the "master stories" of Judaism and Christianity, the Exodus and the passion-resurrection, are the most familiar common memories in America's congregations. Although Islamic and Buddhist congregations may tell other stories, the function of common memory is much the same.

Obviously, congregations are not the only institutions that have common memories. The Rotary Club, the Democratic Party, and Great Britain all possess shared memories. But congregations are distinguished by the particular memories they cherish. They pledge allegiance to a fundamental story, rehearsing it again and again. Indeed, congregations are the only institutions in the American context where, week in and week out, everyday people voluntarily assemble around particular *religious* stories.

These master stories shape common memories in a variety of ways. Most American congregations follow some sort of liturgical calendar, whether it be high or low church. At worship, in pastoral care, at key moments of life's passage, in meetings, and in programs of mission, congregations also mediate their stories.

Granted, congregations do not transmit only their master stories. At church suppers, in congregational meetings, even at worship, master stories and local tales intermingle. At times the master story seems to disappear from congregational recall. On other occasions, the master story is retold with amazing simplicity and directness. But it always exists in a complex narrative relation with other stories that are part of its environment.

Moreover, master stories themselves, in the late twentieth century, are problematic for many. Biblical scholars revise our interpretations, feminists recast Christianity with more inclusive imagery, Hispanics and blacks seek alternative versions to the established Protestant, Catholic, and Jewish renditions that exclude them. On the one hand, such responses are signs that master stories still matter, that people take them seriously enough to contend over them. On the other hand, contemporary narrative controversy is a sign that other master stories are getting a hearing within the American context, an indicator of the flourishing pluralism that places strains on any storytelling community. Common memories are becoming less common—a sign, perhaps, of encroaching amnesia.

Before turning attention to congregational amnesia, however, it is important to note several other features about these communities of memory. First, as the Jewish and Christian scriptures remind us, the great religious traditions have always placed a great value on memory. Moses commanded Israel to remember, and Passover, wilderness experience, and God's mighty acts of deliverance are still recalled by a people that remembers the Sabbath and all the other parts of the Jewish story. For Christians, a parallel command to remember is heard at Jesus' last supper: "Do this in remembrance of me." Both of these religious founders linked salvation and memory, and thus the rituals, scriptures, cultic leaders, and institutions that followed these seminal commands all emerged out of a primal commitment to remember.

More was going on in these acts of memory than mere recollection of past events. In the Christian understanding of *anamnesis* (remembrance), for example, there is the potent idea that in the gathered community's liturgical retelling of God's mighty acts, the past is re-presented, Moses or Jesus come to life again in this new moment, and the saving presence of God is encountered. In other words, memory bridges the gap between past, present, and (given the eschatological character of Judaism and Christianity) future. Thus memory is not optional for congregations. Their very lives depend upon their ability to recall and transmit.

Second, what keeps a common memory common is what Gustafson called its "center." His focus was on the Christian church, so it comes as little surprise that he identified Jesus Christ as the center that gave the church's memory its distinctiveness and its coherence. Different congregations can exist around different centers. But it is doubtful whether a congregation, a community of common memory, can exist for long where no center can be found. Each congregation needs a common memory if it is to endure. In one way or another a congregation must relate members toward that center so as to build an identity or character that is more than a passing fancy.

Finally, centered common memories can take a great variety of shapes. For example, within the Christian stream there are Protestant, Catholic, and Orthodox versions. Within Protestantism there are Episcopalian, Reformed, Anabaptist, and Lutheran subplots. Within the Lutheran episode one finds German and Scandinavian versions. Within the German strand come pietist and rationalist movements. The rationalist stream can have its evangelical and legalistic parties. And the legalistic party can have its Ohio and its Arizona chapters. Alongside Catholicism, Orthodoxy, and Judaism, other streams within Protestantism can easily provide countless analogies to this pattern. Yet somehow, in the midst of all the variety and choice borne along by tradition, a continuity with the center endures. It is this powerful commitment to stay in touch with particular yet ultimate life-giving centers that sets congregations apart from other institutions in American life. But the pull to the center is only one part of the American congregational story.

## Places of Amnesia

Perhaps no American exemplifies the centrifugal dimension of the American character more forcefully than Henry Ford, the man who put Americans behind the wheel. When he stated in a 1916 *Chicago Tribune* interview that "history is more or less bunk," the inventor of the automobile, the assembly line, and installment payments reduced a mind-set to an aphorism. The America he valued was a place where new things could happen. Like the highway billboards that soon became part of Ford's legacy, remnants of the past cluttered the highway of American inventiveness. In his unsophisticated way, Ford expressed something that seems to be essential for Americans: a yearning to break free from the bonds of the past and a relentless search for new experiences of self-realization.

On a different scale our national political life manifests a type of amnesia about the past that is the other side of the intentional forgetting championed by Ford. When historian Daniel Boorstin (1953:33) surveyed the history of our political institutions and compared them with those of Europe he found that "we Americans are reared with a feeling for the unity of our history and an unprecedented belief in the normality of our kind of life to our place on earth." As a rule Americans look at their way of life and see it as inevitable, a self-evident reality that just seems to fit.

In the thirty-five years since Boorstin made his observations about the common American memory, we have become a bit more skeptical about the fit between our political institutions and our current situation. But the amnesia so intriguing to Boorstin still remains an essential part of the American character. By blotting out the complexity of our pluriform pasts, our amnesia facilitates the individualistic quest that seems to be the center of our life together. Whether such an egocentric center can hold in a time of deepening pluralism is of course the great question lurking beneath our various political contests and controversies. Such doubts have recently occasioned much self-examination by American scholars, producing such books as Robert Bellah's *Habits of the Heart: Individualism and Community in American Life* (1985). But the unintended importance of amnesia for our way of life must not be underestimated. As a people we value not memory but freedom from it.

History, the discipline of critical reflection upon the past, enters the interplay between memory and amnesia as an essential third force, revising the former and undermining the latter. Through a variety of means, the historian enriches our memories. Where our recall is less than total, the historian recovers additional evidence and fills in. Where our memories distort the past, limit the present, and foreclose the future, historians correct our selective vision and provide room for new possibilities to emerge. When we lose our sense of who we are, when amnesia and disorientation prevail over memory, history makes possible the reconstruction of identities appropriate to changing circumstances. Memory is a precious, if at times deceptive, resource for historians. Amnesia is history's foil. Rather than leave people in the aimlessness of amnesia, the historian renders the past present, and then makes intentional judgments about which parts of the past are useful in present situations and which are not.

With this relationship between memory, amnesia, and history in view, we now turn to a historical case study of one congregation that may shed light on how other congregations have remembered and forgotten their pasts and how these acts of memory and amnesia have influenced their subsequent institutional lives.

## City Church

In 1926, the nineteen-year-old First Methodist Church of Gary, Indiana, took the name "City Church." The new name proved to be central to the young congregation's self-definition and subsequent institutional memory.[1] City Church had grown up simultaneously along with the new city of Gary, founded in 1906 by U.S. Steel. Like new churches elsewhere in the United States, City Church devoted its early years to survival, organization, and building.

Its second pastor, Joseph Avann, led the new congregation into a period of relative prosperity and prominence in its rapidly urbanizing setting. During his influential five-year pastorate (1911–1916) the elderly Avann and his wife dedicated themselves to the nurture of the young congregation. But they also took seriously the needs of the young city and supported the laity of the congregation in responding to those needs. For example, the Women's Home Missionary Society of the church established a mission Sunday School and day nursery in February 1913 in order to minister to the needs of Gary's rapidly growing immigrant population.[2] By 1914 these efforts developed into the Campbell Friendship House, which was for many years an important part of the church's ministry to the immigrant, and later the black, population of Gary.

Avann also initiated efforts to establish a Protestant system of "released time" religious education in conjunction with the public schools. Upon learning that some Jewish children in Gary spent part of their school day receiving religious instruction in the synagogue, Avann sought a similar arrangement for the Protestant students. After securing the approval of the superintendent of schools, William Wirt, and the support of the Pastors' Union, Avann led the initial Protestant efforts to provide religious instruction during the school day in Gary. Although relatively few immigrant children participated in them, the church schools sought to Americanize and Protestantize the immigrant. They were a form of cooperative mission outreach by Gary's Protestants to their non-Protestant neighbors. Under Avann's successor, William Grant Seaman, who served from 1916 to 1929, these early efforts evolved into a full-blown system of weekday church schools that consciously served as a model for similar Protestant initiatives around the country (J. Lewis, 1987:121–131; see also Squires, 1919).

Avann's early efforts, then, impressed upon the young congregation the necessity of ministering to the boisterous new city of which it was a part. It was a lasting legacy, and Avann's successor, William Grant Seaman, later praised his ministry as one of "marked efficiency" (cited in J. Lewis, 1987:270). When Avann died in 1916 at age sixty-five (the first minister to die in the ten-year-old city), the *Gary Tribune* (June 6, 1916) lionized him as a prominent citizen whose work had "placed the First Methodist among the leaders of religious thought of this growing population."

From an early date, then, First Methodist Church participated prominently in Gary's municipal life, a tradition that reached its peak in the next decade and a half under the leadership of William Grant Seaman. Seaman, a fifty-year-old philosophy professor, college president, and minister, came to Gary convinced that Protestant churches should play an important role in the modern city.[3]

Seaman did not, of course, develop his position on the urban church in a vacuum. Indeed his thinking clearly reflects the social gospel movement of the late nineteenth and early twentieth centuries, which emphasized Protestant responsibility for building the kingdom of God, even in the midst of modern industrial society. To the serious challenge presented by the modern city, advocates of the social gospel proposed, among other remedies, municipal political reform, social settlement houses, and so-called institutional churches, which provided a multitude of services to the city's diverse population.

An heir of the social gospel, Seaman also built on the activist past of his own congregation. In particular, he praised Avann's "aggressive spirit for the promotion of the Kingdom" and his establishment of the weekday church schools, to which Seaman in turn devoted so much of his own time (J. Lewis, 1987:269). Seaman brought together the vision of the social gospel and the tradition of his own congregation, carrying the dream of progressive urban Protestantism beyond World War I to the eve of the Depression decade.

Early in his pastorate Seaman astutely analyzed Gary's social problems and proposed systematic strategies to address several of them, including inadequate health care, racial and ethnic hostility, and rapid population mobility. Central to his vision of an aggressive urban Protestantism was a multipurpose downtown church building dedicated to service to the whole city. Adroitly working with both denominational and U.S. Steel officials (including Judge Elbert Gary, Chairman of the Board), Seaman managed to construct a $777,000 social gospel cathedral in downtown Gary, with U.S. Steel donating half the cost. The building was dedicated with great fanfare on October 3, 1926, and from that day on First Methodist was known as City Church. Its motto (proudly displayed both on the dedication program and on church bulletins thereafter) was: "That Christ May Dwell, a Living Presence, at the City's Heart."

Both the church's new name and its motto summarized Seaman's vision for urban Protestantism—a Protestantism at the heart of the city. But one generation's vision is another generation's memory, and Seaman's complex vision for City Church, reflecting broader Christian history, the American social gospel, and the particular history of First Methodist Church, became integral to the congregation's central institutional memory. At once, the social gospel cathedral in Gary reflected both the centuries-old notion of an urban cathedral and the construction in the nineteenth and twentieth centuries of prominent downtown churches in many American cities (Chicago's Methodist Temple, for example). The congregation's motto, "That Christ May Dwell, a Living Presence, at the City's Heart," revealed both Seaman's and the social gospel's vision of the church at the center. But it also harked back to the characteristic Methodist emphasis on heartfelt religion, dating back to John Wesley himself.

Subsequent generations remembered, forgot, and retrieved that complex vision of City Church in a variety of ways and in the midst of changing historical circumstances. By the 1960s and 1970s, a church's location at the center of the city (an "inner-city" church) had very different connotations than it had in the 1920s (a "downtown" church). Memories of past vitality and influence were replaced by daily reminders of decline and irrelevance, and Seaman's vision of City Church no longer enjoyed the shaping power over congregational life it had in an earlier generation.

But for Seaman in the 1910s and 1920s, building the church downtown was essential for at least two reasons. First, a central location placed the church on a par with other downtown institutions of citywide influence. As he said:

> The whole city needs the "Down-Town Church." At the heart of the city are those institutions that stand for universal needs, the store, the bank, the professional office, the theatre. The Church should be there too, in a strong way sending out its healing influence to every part of the city.

Although he would not have put it quite this way, Seaman felt that to put the church on the periphery was to make it peripheral. Said Seaman, "We cannot save the world without saving the cities and we cannot save the cities without saving them at the heart."[4]

Second, the church should be at the center of the city in order to fulfill its mission to the center. On the one hand, many of the evils to be fought were located there, including "the strongholds of ignorance, immorality, crime, disease," as well as "debasing amusements, low theatres, immoral dance halls" (Seaman, 1920a:4). On the other hand, many of the groups to which the church needed to minister were located there as well, including businessmen, foreigners, transients, young people rooming away from home, and so forth (Seaman, 1923:2–3). Once located at the center, the church should offer a program calculated to minister to the city's many needs. On several occasions Seaman described this program as follows:

> From the heart of a city radiates its life and influence. That is why our church was put where it is. Then came the plan of service, a plan for a church open seven days a week, a church presenting the beautiful in music and architecture, a church providing Christian educational features, healthful recreation, appealing and clean entertainment for youth and age, and above all, a church spreading by deed and word the spirit of Christian friendliness.[5]

For a variety of reasons, among them the onset of the Depression, Seaman and City Church did not realize their dream. But they did, at their best, render an effective ministry to the young city of Gary during the 1910s and 1920s.

Seaman's vision survived his 1929 departure from the congregation, but it was remembered and appropriated in a variety of ways over the years. In the 1930s the vision of a vital city church gave way to the imperatives of institutional survival in a depression decade. But ministers in the 1940s (William Clark) and 1950s (Elbert Cole) attempted to revive Seaman's vision of City Church as they sought to lead the congregation into greater service to the city. Like Seaman before him, William Clark (pastor from 1932 to 1946) sought in the 1940s to lead the church to take an active role in the life of the city. For example, he worked actively on behalf of improved race relations and sought to improve the artistic and cultural life of Gary (J. Lewis, 1987:334–335). In a letter four decades later (Clark to Lewis, December 20, 1984), Clark said:

> I tried to keep the dream of City Church alive and well in the day that then was and under the prevailing conditions. History will have to be the judge of that. It was a great day to be alive!

After Clark, however, the central memory of City Church seemed to fade as membership declined precipitously from its peak of 3,185 in 1952. It was the not inconsiderable accomplishment of Elbert Cole to halt this decline and even reverse it slightly during his four years in Gary (1955–1959). He brought to Gary a concept of the role of the church in the industrial city that was reminiscent of that held by William Grant Seaman four decades earlier, but which also reflected changes since the 1920s (J. Lewis, 1987:340). But apparently it was not a vision shared widely by the membership. Despite the beautiful building and the presence in the church of strong lay leadership, Cole felt that the congregation had, in many ways, lost its vision as a city church (J. Lewis, 1987:341). Amnesia, or at least blurred vision, had set in.

In the late 1950s, however, Gary's Methodist churches were thriving, at least in the suburbs, and there was little sense of white flight or urban decline in the central city. Employment in the mills remained high, and Gary remained prosperous to all appearances.

But rapid change was in fact at the door. Even before Gary's often cited racial change, a report by the Indiana Council of Churches painted a somber picture of the future of Gary's downtown Protestant churches (Kelley and Greene, 1964). Although 1960 census figures reveal few blacks in the census tract containing City Church, rapid racial change was well under way by 1970 (J. Lewis, 1987:342).[6] Despite attempts in the 1960s under S. Walton Cole (minister 1964–1970; no relation to Elbert Cole) to minister to the church's new black and Hispanic neighbors, the rapid decline of City Church continued.[7] The formerly grand building required increasing levels of maintenance at a time of inadequate financial resources. Younger members moved to Gary's new suburbs, leaving an aging congregation in an aging building. A new population—generally poorer and black or Hispanic—brought alternative memories of other congregational traditions, memories not easily integrated with those of City Church. A whole cluster of factors contributed to the church's changed situation, and by the 1970s the congregation saw itself not as a strategic church at the center but as a beleaguered institution in a threatening inner city. It appears that the rapid pace of social change in Gary alongside, perhaps, the congregation's loss of vision, overwhelmed the church's ability to adapt. In light of these new social circumstances, the memory of a vital City Church persisted only as a reminder of what once had been.

When Floyd Blake became pastor in 1972 some members assumed he had been sent by the bishop to close City Church, a charge Blake denied. Attending to the future of the church was his main task, to which he devoted seventy to eighty percent of his time during his first six months. His study of the situation even included trips to other inner-city congregations around the country. His conclusions were stark. City Church had failed to adapt in time to its black and Hispanic neighbors, and its opportunity for ministry to them had passed. Sounding not unlike Seaman, Blake said, "You must serve the changing community as it changes and you must serve it with flexible changing methods or there comes a time when it is too late!" As for City Church: "We have waited too long. It is too late to do our dreams" (J. Lewis, 1987:347). Blake left in 1973, and in 1975, like many another downtown church, City Church closed its doors forever.

In many ways, Seaman's carefully articulated 1920s vision of a church at the vital city center made little sense in an urban America that was moving pell-mell to the suburbs. Historians David Goldfield and Blaine Brownell claim that the "radiant center" image of the city, which emphasized the centrality of downtown, reached its zenith in America in the 1920s and declined thereafter (Goldfield and Brownell 1979:292–293). If they are correct, by the time that City Church's grand building was completed in Gary's downtown, the vitality of American cities had already begun to shift from center to periphery. Within a few years, City Church's identity no longer fit the reality of its urban environment.

In the case of City Church, then, the memory of the church at the center may well have been inadequate for Gary in the 1960s and 1970s. But by then, of course, the memory had faded anyway in the corporate mind of the congregation. What is more, since the present is never quite like the past, even if it had been revived it might have made little difference.

But that is not to say that the congregation's failure to remember was unimportant. To return once more to James Gustafson, the past "that was important enough to be remembered and expressed has contemporary significance as well" (Gustafson, 1985:82). Historian Bernard Lewis reminds us that history (remembered, recovered, and invented, as he says) can be selective with a purpose. As the Jews did with the memory of the heroic battle of Masada, a people can sometimes retrieve a long-forgotten event in the service of a new reality in the present (B. Lewis, 1987). It is just possible, then, that City Church's vision, appropriated for a new age, might have made a difference. But "might have beens" are uncomfortable territory for the historian. Suffice it to say that the congregation's amnesia in the 1960s and 1970s robbed it, at the very least, of one *possible* resource of new vitality. More than that the historian cannot say.

Historian Jay Dolan has noted that "people can never understand who they are unless they understand who they were" (Dolan, 1987:I:1). Likewise congregations need to remember their past and allow that memory to inform and enrich the present. Such memory of the past may offer new imaginative possibilities to a congregation. But the limits of memory must also be kept in mind as congregations move from the past toward the future. History can be used; it cannot be repeated.

## Implications for Congregations

1. If congregations are communities of memory, then congregational history ceases to be a quaint topic to be farmed out to anniversary committees and retirees with time on their hands. Instead, the methods of the historian become an important resource for identifying, understanding, and making use of congregational memory. They are essential for overcoming amnesia, correcting selective vision, distinguishing between tradition and traditionalism.

Congregations develop their own ways of life, and each bears a particular ethos. To appreciate that ethos clergy and congregational members together must develop skills and perspectives that can help it come into view.[8] They need to consider, for example, their congregation's distinctive setting. Is it urban? rural? suburban? Are its members principally middle-class, upper-class, lower-class? Does it have a tradition of strong pastoral leadership, strong lay leadership, or both? Such contextual particulars matter in the history of a congregation just as particulars matter in the biography of an individual. Moreover such particulars constitute filaments of memory that inform a congregation's life in important and complex ways.

Congregations are seldom aware of all their memories, or of the thickness of the ways of life they have developed. Part of a congregation's task is to discover its past, to revalue its identity and experience. This reperception can provide new shared understandings that can contribute to a new congregational sense of purpose and vitality. As common memory is forged, a common language and common symbols emerge for a stronger community life. Whether continuing a tradition or embarking upon a new direction, awakened memory can be a powerful resource.

Amnesia, on the other hand, severely limits the imaginative repertoire of a congregation. With no shared images, congregations are left with little to guide or inspire. Thus congregational history becomes a resource for pastors, enabling them better to understand the distinctive setting of their ministries. At the same time it also opens up new shared perspectives that can allow the congregation itself to deepen its sense of mission.

2. Our memory does play tricks on us. We have habits of thought that we do not notice. Frequently we label as "traditional" rather recent innovations. Often we turn around and make the opposite mistake, identifying a behavior or belief an "innovation" when in fact it may be an expression of an earlier but forgotten part of our past. As psychologists have taught us about our personal memories, so congregational historians can help us learn about the powerful ways in which repressed memories shape our life. The pain of a congregational schism, the feelings of betrayal remaining after a pastor suddenly resigns, the cynicism lingering after a congregational scandal, and many other memories often go unmentioned in daily congregational discourse. Yet those repressed memories, hiding under the facade of amnesia, can powerfully shape a community's life.

So we need to be careful with congregational memories. People's deepest values are tangled up in them. And often they can be deceptive. We also need to watch out for amnesia in our religious conventional wisdom. By and large, historians and church people as well have forgotten there was a time when mainstream Protestants unapologetically and rather heroically sought to be (and to an extent succeeded in being) urban Christians. We have too readily accepted the stereotyped notion that American Protestantism is intrinsically rural and (in our day) suburban. We have forgotten churches that in the late nineteenth and (as in Gary) the first third of our own century did not regard the phrase "urban Protestant" as a contradiction in terms. Our amnesia concerning our urban past has, perhaps, made us all too willing to accept as inevitable the decline of mainstream Protestantism in the inner city of the late twentieth century. America's cities are indeed a monumental challenge to religious institutions of many kinds. But to remember that there was a time (not so long ago) when mainstream Protestants could give allegiance to the notion "that Christ may dwell, a Living Presence, at the city's heart" is to be reminded that religious traditions represent a rich and many-layered source of human wisdom and creativity that need not accept despair meekly, even in the modern city. Such memories also remind us of the value of recovering the histories of particular congregations whose urban experience can teach us much even today.

3. Here is where the real practical character of congregational history becomes clearest. If people are shaping their life together on the basis of flawed, incomplete, false, or unreal memories, then those memories need uncovering and healing. A congregation's history thus becomes a matter of mutuality. We all have flawed memories and need the corrective perspectives that come only from others who share our history. Thus congregational history can become a corporate form of pastoral care where people help each other see things and themselves more clearly and more completely. Truth is not handed down unchanged from solitary authority figures on high. It is discovered anew in a common search for shared identity and understanding. In the process of finding larger relations, of seeing how individual experience connects with a congregation's little and great traditions, people may discover a larger wholeness than they knew previously. To restrict congregational history to occasional anniversary celebrations or to the first months of a new pastorate is to under-utilize a precious resource.

Instead, serious exploration of congregational history can create opportunities for people to tell and retell their congregational stories. As shared understandings emerge, it becomes possible to tell the more difficult parts of a community's story and for its healing to begin. To fail to explore the congregation's common memory is to risk leaving wounds festering beneath the surface, a strategy that will backfire when a new congregational controversy occurs. Exploring the history of a congregation becomes a way to create room for a congregation to move on with its life—with a clearer sense of who it has been and is, as well as a fresh appreciation of itself as a trustworthy community that can deal with its human failings.

4. Congregational history makes it possible for churches and synagogues to challenge the throwaway mind-set of our culture. As antique collectors remind us, there are things worth saving from the past. Exploring parish or synagogue history can help people learn skills that may help with our larger cultural amnesia problem. While few of us want to be Luddites who oppose whatever is new, our nation's own problems with the memory-amnesia dynamic suggest that a much greater adeptness at relating past and present is needed than we can individually muster. Congregations could thus become houses of historical perspective that can contribute a richer repertoire of imaginative possibility to our current problems.

5. If the need to facilitate and deepen memory is genuine, as we clearly believe it is, then those who lead congregations need to learn how to read an additional set of texts besides those that receive so much attention in the seminary curriculum. While in no way suggesting that sacred scriptures, confessional writings, theological texts, and the like should be slighted, we do intend to point to the congregation as a text—a living one—that requires interpretive skill. Certainly historical perspective is important for such reading. But so are insights from social sciences, theology, and organizational dynamics.

6. If congregations need to become better able to explore their own memories, then the institutions that train their clergy and support them in their ministries need to foster these abilities. Seminaries need to turn attention not only to their sacred texts and the various official skills that allow pastors to function professionally. They also must help pastors learn how to approach a congregation and interpret its life. Every pastor, priest, or rabbi should in some sense become a congregational historian. Denominations also need to move beyond their current patterns of relating to congregations. If pastors are to take seriously the distinctiveness of congregations and discover the central role they play, then denominations will need to begin to reexplore their own identities and histories in ways that allow congregational dimensions to come to the fore.

7. Finally, if pastors, congregations, denominations, and seminaries begin to appreciate the significance of the treasure contained in congregational memories, then perhaps our larger interpretations of American religion and society can begin to make room for local memories that may be quite at odds with national ones. These, like the memory of City Church, may challenge conventional wisdom, which assigns congrega-

tional life to the periphery, leaving American life quite hollow at the center.

## NOTES

1. This brief account of City Church is based on James W. Lewis, "At Home in the City: Mainstream Protestantism in Gary, Indiana, 1906–1983" (Ph.D. dissertation, University of Chicago, 1987).

2. By November 1908, according to Graham R. Taylor, Gary's population of 10,246 included representatives of no fewer than twenty-four nationalities and was over 60 percent foreign. See Graham R. Taylor, *Satellite Cities: A Study of Industrial Suburbs* (New York: D. Appleton & Co., 1915), p. 196.

3. Bishop Thomas Nicholson of Chicago, who had "a warm personal interest in Chicago's new industrial neighbor Gary," worked closely with the congregation in the selection of Seaman, after a long and careful search. Nicholson, like Seaman, advocated an activist Protestant presence in the city. See William F. Switzer, "Notes for Gary First Methodist Church History" (1934), p. 4, Gary–City United Methodist Collection, Document Case 116, Archives of DePauw University and Indiana United Methodism, Greencastle, Indiana.

4. "Program of the Methodist Episcopal Church, Gary, Indiana." Although not signed by him, this document was almost certainly written by William Grant Seaman around 1920. It may be found in the Gary–City United Methodist Collection in the Archives of DePauw University and Indiana United Methodism, Greencastle, Indiana. The second quote is from another such document surely written by Seaman, "What the Centenary Has Done," p. 3 (also in the archives at DePauw University).

5. Quoted in *Gary Post-Tribune*, October 15, 1926.

6. This report confirmed that, although there were few black residents of the census tract in which City Church was located, dilapidation of the housing stock there had already begun to occur. See Arleon Kelley and Wilma Greene, *Reconnaissance Study of the Inner City: Gary, Indiana* (Indianapolis: Indiana Council of Churches, 1964), pp. 41–51.

7. Blacks had never constituted a significant part of City Church membership. Presumably they rarely felt welcome there. But in addition, Gary had several large black Methodist churches, including Trinity Methodist Episcopal Church (established 1917), which cooperated with City Church over the years (Lewis, 1987:295).

8. A resource that provides several different perspectives on congregational history is James P. Wind, *Places of Worship: Exploring their History* (Nashville: American Association for State and Local History, 1990).

## WORKS CITED

Bellah, Robert N., and Richard Madsen, William M. Sullivan, Ann Swidler, and Stephen M. Tipton
    1985      *Habits of the Heart: Individualism and Commitment in American Life.* Berkeley, Calif.: University of California Press.

Boorstin, Daniel J.
1953 *The Genius of American Politics.* Chicago: University of Chicago Press.

Dolan, Jay P. (ed.)
1987 *The American Catholic Parish: A History from 1850 to the Present.* 2 vols. Mahwah, N.J.: Paulist Press.

Goldberg, Michael
1985 *Jews and Christians: Getting Our Stories Straight.* Nashville: Abingdon Press.

Goldfield, David R. and Blaine A. Brownell
1979 *Urban America: From Downtown to No Town.* Boston: Houghton Mifflin Co.

Gustafson, James M.
1985 *Treasure in Earthen Vessels.* New York: Harper & Row, 1961; reprint ed., Chicago: University of Chicago Press, Midway Reprint.

Kelley, Arleon, and Wilma Greene
1964 *Reconnaissance Study of the Inner City: Gary, Indiana.* Indianapolis: Indiana Council of Churches.

Lewis, Bernard
1987 *History: Remembered, Recovered, Invented.* New York: Simon & Schuster, Touchstone. First published by Princeton University Press, 1975.

Lewis, James
1987 "At Home in the City: Mainstream Protestantism in Gary, Indiana, 1906–1983." Ph.D. dissertation, University of Chicago.

Seaman, William G.
c. 1920a "Program of the Methodist Episcopal Church." Gary, Indiana. Gary–City United Methodist Collection in the Archives of DePauw University and Indiana United Methodism, Greencastle, Indiana.
c. 1920b "What the Centenary Has Done." Gary–City United Methodist Collection in the Archives of DePauw University and Indiana United Methodism, Greencastle, Indiana.
c. 1923 "First Methodist Episcopal Church, Gary, Indiana." Gary–City United Methodist Collection in the Archives of DePauw University and Indiana United Methodism, Greencastle, Indiana.
n.d. "Romance of City Church Architecture." Gary–City United Methodist Collection in the Archives of DePauw University and Indiana United Methodism, Greencastle, Indiana.

Squires, Walter A.
1919 *The Gary Plan of Church Schools.* Philadelphia: Presbyterian Board of Publication and Sabbath School Work.

Wind, James P.
1990 *Places of Worship: Exploring Their History.* Nashville: American Association for State and Local History.

# TWO

# The Changing Context of Parish Leadership
## DAVID C. LEEGE

Catholics in the United States are the products of two ecclesiastical traditions. The one, dominant from the 1830s to the 1950s, saw the parish as the priest writ large. He was sacramental minister, preacher, spiritual counselor, comforter of the sick, the primary teacher, presider at communion breakfasts, chaplain to all parish societies, supervisor of youth athletics, and trainer of altar boys (Dolan, 1989). In many dioceses, the priest could even treat parish incomes as a personal benefice at his disposal. If he had help, it was in the persons of women members of religious orders, or other priests subject to his authority. He acted as the representative of the bishop.

Prior to the 1830s, a still older tradition lodged heavy responsibility for the parish in the laity. Lay trustees organized parishes, owned church property, ran financial affairs, and made requests to the diocese or foreign mission societies for priests. Sometimes there were squabbles between the laity and priests on the question: Whose parish is this? The trustee system was widely discouraged as the American bishops consolidated control over the presbytery (Dolan, 1985). Nowadays it is typically perceived as a Protestant form of governance.

These two traditions operate in a different manner in contemporary parish experience. What is characteristic of the modern American parish is that "leadership" is a plural noun. While the pastor is still central, there are many other influential and effective people who share responsibility for the direction of the parish. In the post–Vatican II American church, that is both by necessity and design. For, at about the time that social and psychological forces made the priesthood a less attractive vocation for young men, the Catholic Church itself was urging the nonordained to share more widely the ministries and responsibilities of the parish.

Norms derived from American culture, current canon law, and great demographic differences have yielded complex local leadership structures.

The Notre Dame Study of Catholic Parish Life, from whose data much of this chapter is drawn,[1] illustrates how the context for Catholic parish leadership has been substantially altered by four forces: (1) the increasing demand for parish services; (2) the declining supply of priests and members of religious communities, such as sisters; (3) enormous demographic changes within the membership, particularly in education, suburbanization, gender roles, and gaps between the rich and the poor, that have led to a new sense of lay responsibility; and (4) a post–Vatican II ecclesiology that emphasizes the church as "the people of God" and the "ordination of baptism." The ordination of baptism stresses that all baptized laity have responsibilities to build God's kingdom in church and culture. While this ordination does not include the unique sacramental and pastoral duties of a priest, it is nevertheless a call to active participation.

Catholic parishes that successfully respond to these forces enjoy a strong sense of community and parishioner loyalty. But the response is uneven and is most often problematic in parishes of town and countryside, where priests often act as they did in earlier times. Nevertheless, aside from limitations of parish size and location, few parishes are straitjacketed by the social characteristics of their parishioners; leaders *can* make a difference, and often parishes make their own destinies. Because forces 1, 3, and 4 are also found in Protestant congregations, even if under other labels, I feel that much of the content of this chapter may be instructive for understanding changes in Protestant congregational leadership as well.

## Demand for Parish Services

In the late 1980s, there were about 19,500 Catholic parishes in the United States. Based on parish censuses and local estimating procedures, there were about 53 million Catholics. General population surveys are now finding that about 28 percent of respondents claim to be Catholics, suggesting that there may be as many as 70 million Catholics in the country. As with any American church, it is reasonable to assume that a substantial proportion of people who claim cultural connection with the church are not known to its local parishes.

### Parish Size and Location

As of 1983, the median Catholic parish had about 2,330 "members." (The concept of "membership" is characteristically American because it connotes voluntary affiliation. The Catholic Church does not use the term, because its parishes are to serve all people, and serve sacramentally those who are Catholics, within a given geographic area. The figure is based on the pastor's or parish administrator's estimate of the Catholic population within the parish.) A little over one-third of the parishes serve 1,000 or fewer people, one-fourth serve 1,000 to 2,500, one-fifth serve 2,500 to 5,000, and the remainder serve 5,000 or more. Catholic parishes are large, perhaps on the average seven to eight times greater than Protestant congregations. In fact, an important finding of the study is that several recognizable "congregations," based on liturgical practices and religious and social needs, exist within each parish.

About 86 percent of American parishes are territorially defined and 10 percent are explicitly based on ministry to a nationality or ethnic group. Clearly, however, in some large cities and other locales, distinct ethnic groups continue to predominate in a territorial parish. Most people think of Catholics as an urban population and, like other upwardly mobile Americans, Catholics experienced much suburbanization. What is more surprising, however, is that 46 percent of all parishes are located outside the metropolitan counties (counties having a central city of greater than 50,000 population); an estimated one-third of all Catholics are located in parishes of town and countryside. That is a nonmetropolitan Catholic population larger than the total membership of either of the two largest Protestant bodies, the Southern Baptists or the United Methodists.

### Expectations for Services

One of the best ways to understand the leadership context of parishes is to explore parishioners' expectations for services the parish should provide. In the American context, local churches have become far more than centers for religious sustenance. That is demonstrated for Catholics in Table 2.1. The table is based on the proportion of parishioners who would turn for help to each source—pastor or parish staff, friends, or professionals outside the parish—for each kind of problem. The fourth column shows the proportion who would turn to the pastor or parish staff if competent help or good programs were available, and the fifth column shows the "opportunity gap" created by the difference between the first and fourth columns.

Beyond Mass or other religious celebrations, nearly all parishioners expect the parish to provide for the religious education of their children and themselves, and most Catholics look to the parish for support for their

**TABLE 2.1**

**Sources of Help for Parishioner Needs**
**(Based on 22,667 Parishioners in 36 Catholic Parishes)**

| Problem | Percentage of respondents who would turn for help to | | | If help were offered within parish, percentage turning to | "Opportunity gap" |
|---|---|---|---|---|---|
| | Pastor, parish staff | Friends | Professionals outside parish | Pastor, parish staff | |
| 1. Religious education of children | 84.4% | 1.3% | 1.8% | 85.8% | 1.4% |
| 2. Religious education for myself | 82.6 | 2.4 | 3.4 | 84.9 | 2.3 |
| 3. Support for faith | 78.3 | 8.5 | 1.2 | 79.4 | 1.1 |
| 4. Premarital counseling or marital renewal | 74.1 | 3.3 | 9.0 | 78.7 | 4.6 |
| 5. Counseling at time of sickness | 53.0 | 18.1 | 19.3 | 63.6 | 10.6 |

| | | | | |
|---|---|---|---|---|
| 6. Opportunities to serve others | 47.9 | 21.3 | 18.3 | 60.2 | 12.3 |
| 7. Death of a member of my family | 46.3 | 43.5 | 3.5 | 48.8 | 2.5 |
| 8. A place to express my doubts and fears without judgment | 44.0 | 34.0 | 11.2 | 49.0 | 5.0 |
| 9. Severe marital problems | 39.2 | 11.4 | 36.9 | 59.6 | 20.4 |
| 10. Family problems | 36.5 | 24.2 | 26.3 | 51.0 | 14.5 |
| 11. Unwanted pregnancy | 31.8 | 13.9 | 34.9 | 46.7 | 14.9 |
| 12. Handling of painful memories | 30.4 | 42.5 | 16.0 | 38.7 | 8.3 |
| 13. Alcohol/drug abuse | 13.3 | 7.2 | 67.3 | 49.9 | 36.6 |
| 14. Severe money problems | 6.5 | 28.3 | 52.6 | 26.1 | 19.6 |
| 15. Unemployment | 4.9 | 25.3 | 56.4 | 29.6 | 24.7 |

faith and family formation (problems 1 through 4); there is little opportunity gap, since parishes apparently meet these needs. Problems 5 through 12 represent less severe emotional and spiritual traumas—meaning, being needed, separation, intimacy—and about one-half to one-third of parishioners would turn to parish staff for them. The opportunity gap is quite large for severe marital and family problems, counseling situations and, interestingly, the opportunity to serve others, suggesting that parishes are not meeting these expectations as well. Few people turn to parish leaders for alcohol or drug abuse or financial and employment problems (problems 13 through 15); yet, between one-fourth and one-half of parishioners would like to have competent help or good programs available in such areas.

The kinds of parishioners who would turn to parish staff and programs for less severe emotional and spiritual traumas are primarily the younger and moderately educated parishioners and black Catholics. Those who would like to turn to them for severe problems are more likely women of lower income from both the towns and large cities. Highly educated, higher income suburbanites, particularly those with minor children, have grown accustomed to seeking help outside the parish for both mild and severe problems and, therefore, have fewer expectations for such parish services. Otherwise, parishioners differ little in their expectations for the traditional religious education, faith support, and family formation programs (Leege, 1986a:5–6).

*Availability of Parish Services*

The expectations and the reality are two different matters. Table 2.2, based on the sample of nearly 1,100 parishes, shows what proportions of parishes actually have organized programs to meet various expectations.

There is no question that some parishioners' needs are poorly met. General population surveys point out that about one-fourth of all Catholics who have ever married have experienced at least one divorce or separation. Divorce knows no class, region, or local boundaries; it is present in every parish. Yet only 20 percent of the parishes offer programs aimed at the divorced and separated. Women who head households often enter poverty following a divorce, but few parishes have social service programs to tide them over their financial and employment problems. Ironically, the huge affluent suburban parishes with their complex organizational structures are most able to respond to such needs.

The Notre Dame study developed a typology of parish organizational structure ranging from the simplest to the most complex service structure

TABLE 2.2

# Organized Programs in Catholic Parishes in the United States

| Program or activity | *Percentage of parishes having program* |
|---|---|
| **1. Religious education** | |
| elementary level | 93% |
| high school level | 84 |
| adult | 63 |
| parochial school | 45 |
| **2. Liturgy, sacramental life, spirituality** | |
| liturgy planning group | 72 |
| music and cultural activities | 49 |
| prayer, reflection small groups | 46 |
| ministry training programs | 37 |
| catechumenate (RCIA) | 32 |
| evangelization | 32 |
| parish renewal | 29 |
| charismatic renewal | 23 |
| **3. Special ministry through the life cycle** | |
| care of sick | 71 |
| youth | 62 |
| aged | 59 |
| marriage/family development | 48 |
| divorced/separated | 20 |
| **4. Other social ministry** | |
| social service (individual needs) | 52 |
| social action (social change) | 20 |
| **5. Parish governance, decision-making** | |
| parish council | 76 |
| parish planning process | 34 |
| parish leadership training | 27 |
| parish consultant | 19 |

(Leege, 1986a: 8–10). Generally, parish size and suburban locale were good predictors of organizational complexity. Inevitably, the more complex the parish's organizational structure, the higher the likelihood that it would have an active parish council, structures for parish planning and leadership training, and sometimes extraparish instruments—for example, consultants—for goal-setting and conflict resolution.

Complexity and bureaucratization are the English-speaking world's way of dealing with needs. As Catholics enter the American mainstream, it is no coincidence that their parishes move beyond rudimentary programs for religious nurture and expression, to the problem-solving structures designed to rationalize life. The wide range of ministries also testifies to the voluntary nature of American religious organizations: Time after time, parish leaders told us that if the parish could not respond with a specialized ministry, it would lose the loyalties of parishioners to some other local church or voluntary organization.

Such observations foretell a lot about the kinds of people who will become parish leaders, what parishioners will expect about popular consultation on decisions, what kinds of conflicts will develop, and how the local parish's leaders will deal with the diocesan leadership that the Catholic Church has made ecclesiastically responsible for its parishes.

## The Emerging Leaders: Who They Are and How They Act

### Fewer Priests and Religious

If demographic change among parishioners had not altered authority and power relationships within the parish, certainly the supply of priests would have. Several studies (Schoenherr and Sorensen, 1982; Hoge, 1987:3–12) have documented the declining supply of priests and religious, and forecast more of the same but at a rapidly accelerating rate. An estimated 5 percent of the parishes in our study no longer have resident priests, but the proportion of "priestless" parishes in the rural churches is twice as high. Reflecting on the findings, we might even hypothesize that another 15 percent of the parishes are so unfortunately served by their assigned pastor that they might benefit from a well-trained, dedicated, and energetic religious or lay person performing, in effect, as the pastor. Parishes of town and countryside are typically placed at the bottom priority in the assignment pool and are disproportionately assigned priests who were ineffective in larger parishes or suffer burnout, and they experience high turnover among competent men (Burkart and Leege, 1988). Some argue that the Catholic Church's leadership will have to move beyond the consolidation of small parishes toward some significant structural changes in the sanctioning of ministries (Hoge, 1987).

But one should not think of demographic changes among parishioners and the declining supply of priests as distinct trends. They both are symptoms of the same thing—and it has little to do with the lack of dedication to the church. It has much to do with assimilation and, in the future, a component of assimilation—low birthrates. Historically priests have been drawn disproportionately from the middle male children of larger families, often with strong ethnic loyalties (Hoge, Potvin, and Ferry, 1984; Hemrick and Hoge, 1985). Many older ethnic groups have assimilated. More importantly, by the late 1970s, Catholic birthrates declined to the point where Catholic women are having fewer children than Protestant women, even controlling for racial differences (Westoff, 1979; Dolan and Leege, 1986). Hispanics represent the exception to this generalization.

*Emerging Lay Interest and Competence*

Hoge has documented the widespread willingness of Catholics, especially young women, to consider careers in parish professions outside the ordained priesthood or the sisterhood (Hoge, 1987:182-206). Generally lay persons who enter parish professions are highly educated, up to 80 percent are women, and they maintain rather high morale (Walters, 1983; Fox, 1986). Their salaries are much higher than women religious, and cost is often cited by parish pastors as the principal reason for not hiring more lay ministers (Conrad and Shields, 1982:17). But beyond the new class of professionals, many parishes are relying on volunteers to conduct the many ministries cited in Table 2.2.

In recent documents regarding the laity, Catholic leaders are stressing the responsibility that derives from the ordination of baptism. Ordinary Catholic parishioners in the 1980s were uniquely positioned by education, affluence, and outlook to assume parish responsibilities. By the early 1980s, of the major Catholic ethnic groups, only Hispanics and blacks had not exceeded national averages for the completion of college and for family income (Hoge, 1987:51; Greeley, 1985). Catholics tracing lineage to Irish or German parents were well above national norms. The GI Bill had set young Catholic *men* on a course of educational and financial achievement; now both the sons *and* daughters of the World War II generation share these goals. And in the last decade many of their moms were catching up. Throughout recent years, American institutions of higher education have been disproportionately populated by Catholic students (Greeley, 1985).

Education not only changes skills but it also alters outlooks. Already in the 1960s priests and women religious became increasingly "professionalized" as continuing education, sabbaticals, and advanced degree programs overcame the limitations of seminary and convent educations (Dolan, 1989). Sisters, sometimes with more education than priests, began to raise hard questions about the competence of the priest to make some parish decisions. Nowadays, however, lay persons are as well educated as their pastor, if not in religious matters, certainly in organizational development, education and schools, social and psychological services. They expect to be consulted in areas they know something about—and sometimes in areas they know little about. For in America, authority is lodged in the consent of the governed. Further, women's suffrage, access to higher education, the women's movement, and increased experience with economic realities have all contributed to an enhanced sense of competence felt by Catholic *women.*

Our findings demonstrate that larger portions of the parish membership view themselves as qualified for leadership and as community members whose consent on major policy questions must be won. Of those identified as the most influential leaders in the thirty-six-parish intensive study, 83 percent are lay persons and they have normally been in their current parish for about a dozen years, only a couple of years longer than the average parishioner (Leege, 1986b). Lay leaders are almost as mobile as their pastors; only one lay leader in four was raised in his or her current parish. Most arrived there with substantial parish experience: *both* the paid staff and volunteer leaders had, on the average, a dozen years' experience in parish leadership elsewhere. In a sense, each parish is a farm system for another parish's leaders.

Leaders, both paid and volunteer, are better educated than average parishioners; the volunteers have higher incomes, are more deeply enmeshed in friendship networks within the parish, and are more likely than anyone—pastors, paid staff, or parishioners—to be involved in the web of community organizations where they live. They are busy people, thus confirming the adage that if you want to get something done, you ask a busy person.

The emphasis is on "ask." It is a misnomer to say that many of the "volunteers" volunteered. Only 31 percent actually volunteered for their current leadership post; most perceived that they were asked by the pastor or staff to serve. Most pastors tell us that getting a *new* supply of leaders is their most challenging task. Once affirmed in their parish responsibilities, however, lay persons serve with vigor, often spending as many hours on parish matters as do the priest and paid staff.

Even among parishioners not identified as the most influential leaders, parish voluntarism is high. Beyond Mass and devotions, 30 percent of the parishioners who responded to the survey claim to be spending 5 hours per month on parish activities, another 10 percent average 15 hours, 3 percent average 25 hours, and another 2 percent devote virtually all their discretionary hours to the parish (Leege and Trozzolo, 1985:6–7). While social and recreational activities are the most popular, they are nearly matched by lay liturgical roles, such as liturgy planning, choir, lector, or communion minister. Next highest is participation in education and catechesis; governance, finance, and housekeeping; and finally, personal or devotional renewal, social action or social welfare. Slightly over half of all parishioners engage in no organized activities beyond Mass.

Leadership for such a complex range of activities often benefits from in-service training. Training programs are offered by one-fourth to one-third of the parishes. Lay leaders also report extensive use of workshops, retreats, courses, or informal reading of articles or books related to their ministry.

*Decision-Making, Conflict, and Conflict Resolution*

Recent changes in canon law, while still vesting the pastor with authority for the parish, do recognize the need for wider consultation. They mandate parish finance councils and encourage parish councils. At the time of the study, 76 percent of the parishes had a parish council. Three-quarters of the councils met monthly; the remainder, more or less frequently. Most councils include both elected and appointed members, with the pastor typically doing the appointing of staff members to ex officio membership.

Business conducted by the council varies. In the smaller parishes it is often limited to financial matters; in the larger ones the council adopts annual programs and reviews a wide range of parish ministries. Typically pastors use the word "planning" to describe council work, but volunteer leaders are more apt to describe it as "informing" or "reflecting."

Such differences in perception about shared decision-making are reflected in other ways. Pastors, staff, and volunteers agree that financial decisions are shared. Beyond that the pastor typically feels that he shares decision-making for liturgy, parish organizations, social activities, social action, and the school, if there is one. The other leaders seldom share his perception. In particular, the council is thought to be excluded from liturgical planning, which is lodged in the pastor or a liturgy/music director or a small committee. Women who are leaders, in particular, express resentment of the pastor's dominance of the school, parish social activities, and social action efforts.

While 90 percent of the volunteer leaders express confidence that they have access to the pastor, staff, or council, 40 percent of them feel they need more influence. Some dislike clerical dominance, some feel organizations are better served by democratic decision-making, some underscore that talented people are not being consulted, and some are disgruntled about programs, particularly those aimed at liturgy, fostering a sense of parish community, or reaching out to the alienated.

Parish conflict is sometimes healthy, sometimes pathological. The study found that the absence of conflict was more often a sign that the parish was dying or already ossified. Conflict is most likely to occur in parishes of town and countryside where a pastor refuses to share responsibility with others, or where a succession of ineffective pastors for a decade or more has left the parish numb. When conflict occurs, as is reported in three-quarters of the parishes, pastors think it pits the council against the pastor, paid staff think it originates between the pastor and the staff, and volunteer leaders think it comes from a wide variety of sources in the parish. Thus, the position a person occupies in the parish structure leads to different vantage points on conflict.

Position also leads to different perceptions on conflict resolution. Pastors are confident that conflict is resolved through prayer and conversation. Staff think it takes a lot of discussion but conflict is usually resolved with some give and take. Volunteers think the pastor usually gets his way. Despite the presence of conflict, however, pastors, staff, and volunteers offer more positive than negative feelings about one another.

The most discontentment seems to be centered in those positions where expectations have not clearly crystalized. Liturgical musicians seem to be perpetual outsiders, not knowing where they fit in the authority structure and feeling badgered by criticism. Social ministry and social action directors also express frustration in working with the pastor. Although most leaders respect the competence and teamwork of the staff, parish secretaries react more negatively, saying that staff often fail to take the initiative with their own responsibilities or to support others.

Parish council chairs are very sensitive to conflict in the parish but, whether elected or appointed, they often develop close camaraderie with the pastor and see conflict resolution from his perspective. Principals and directors of religious education also come into considerable conflict, typically with the pastor, but they are confident that discussions with him will resolve the conflict to both parties' satisfaction.

The three most distressed leadership positions are typically filled by women. Fifty-eight percent of those named as most influential in the parishes are women. Nevertheless, the *inner circle* of leaders—which we defined as the three people first mentioned as parish leaders by other parish leaders— was 60 percent male and only 40 percent female. Part of the differential, of course, is that in all but a few parishes the pastor, always male, will be in the inner circle. While many women in parish leadership remain deferential to the authority of the pastor and the power of other men, there is no question that they think males use their authority and power over areas of the parish program where they have little understanding.

### Diocesan Relationships

A final element in the context of decision-making in Catholic parishes, often less relevant in Protestant congregations, is diocesan relationships. Once an American hierarchy developed, and control over parishes was consolidated, the bishop and his diocesan staff became potentially significant in every parish. Currently, diocesan involvement is most evident in two ways: (1) the assignment and reassignment of priests/pastors and, to a lesser extent, others who share in the parochial ministry; and (2) the provision of financial resources, parish materials and program aids, consultative services, and leadership training. The latter has become increasingly important as ministries are shared with lay volunteers. The most important symbol of diocesan effectiveness in the future may become the lay ministry training institute, matching the importance of seminaries during the last century and continuing education programs for clergy during the last three decades.

How parish leaders felt about the diocese—or whether they felt anything—again depended on one's vantage point, whether pastor, staff, or volunteer. Feelings among all leadership groups were far more positive than negative. Pastors generally praised the diocese for its moral leadership and educational and training resources. So did staff. Negative comments centered on the siphoning of financial resources from the parish to the diocese, and here, volunteers were particularly vociferous.

For the most part, parochial leaders acted like parochial leaders: their frame of reference is their own parish. When an outside resource is useful, they welcome it; otherwise, they do not want to be bothered. Some, in fact, welcomed their geographic isolation from the diocesan center or the insulation provided by their being served by priests from a religious community.

Those parish leaders who expressed the most frustration—even suffering—were frequently from the smaller parishes of town and countryside. They know their little parish is not a plum, that assignments will sometimes be made from the pool of less effective priests, and even if they get a highly effective priest they will soon lose him to an assignment the diocese considers more challenging. They often accuse the diocesan leadership of having a large-church, suburban bias, and they resent both frequent turnover and the adjustments to priests with very different liturgical and authority styles. They perceive that they are far from the mainstream of Catholic life nowadays in the country, lacking the large pool of educated, skilled, affluent, religiously upbeat parishioners found in metropolitan areas. And they often express resentment over models of the church drawn from that culture. At the same time, they are not Catholic traditionalists; they are far more progressive on church policies and positions than their pastors think they are (Leege and Gremillion, 1986:13). They just wish the diocese would let them get and keep the right priest for a while.

## Leadership and Community

If a successful parish is one that not only spreads the gospel but builds a sense of community and commitment among its members, there are great dividends that come from widespread sharing in parish responsibilities. Nowhere is this more evident than in our data on community and parish loyalty.

The study asked parishioners a variety of questions about the feeling of community in their parish, their sense of attachment to it, the number of close friends they have there, the extent to which it meets their spiritual and social needs, what attracted them to the parish, and how upset they would be about moving from their current parish. We analyzed each of the thirty-six parishes to find out what built the sense of community and commitment. The data are very clear (Leege, 1987).

### Community and Commitment

First, community and commitment are closely related. People who have found community in their parish feel deeply attached to it. Many Catholics want their parishes to be something more than spiritual service stations and will become intensely loyal to a parish that nurtures community. More than one corporate executive told us: "I have passed over promotions in other parts of the country just to stay in this parish."

Secondly, a constellation of parish characteristics predicts community and commitment: (1) the opportunity to participate in parish organizations that serve a wide variety of human needs, (2) responsibility for some part of the parish's life, (3) the quality of the pastor's concern and affirmation, expressed especially by his accessibility and friendliness, (4) the quality of friendliness and concern expressed by fellow parishioners, and (5) liturgies that celebrate the community gathered around the sacrament, that encourage participation in music and liturgical responses, and whose sermons offer insights that can be applied in daily life, rather than withdrawal in anticipation of the afterlife. What is so striking in the data is that the call to common responsibility and service is the principal ingredient in the sense of community and commitment. As anthropologists tell us, what I ought to do (responsibility) derives from who I am (identity). But community does not come without the call to responsibility.

*Sense of Community, Alienation, and Program Support*

Again the finding is sustained by contrasting the parishes with the highest sense of community against the parishes with the lowest sense of community, on their perception of who is alienated. Without exception, the pastors and other leaders in high-community parishes expressed concern about parishioners who came to Mass but did nothing else in the parish. They wanted to deal with "alienation," as they termed it, by the call to greater responsibility. Pastors and other leaders of low-community parishes, on the other hand, were still operating with alienation in terms of conformity to church doctrine, and often its consequences in the life hereafter. Insofar as responsibility mattered for them, it concerned *individual* salvation.

The high-community parishes had twice as many staff members and twice as many volunteer leaders as did the low-community parishes. While there were slight differences in their size, their financial resource bases differed considerably. Financial support in parishes that encourage lay responsibility is much higher. If one compares the economic characteristics of parishioners, their higher financial support is not primarily because the people have more money; rather it stems from their higher level of commitment, and commitment derives from community.

It is equally interesting to note what community does *not* derive from.

In earlier times it was thought that parish community resulted from a common ethnic heritage. While our data show a slight tendency for the ethnically homogeneous parishes to have a higher sense of community, still, three of the four parishes with the strongest sense of community are ethnically heterogenous. Neither does parish size nor urban-rural location predict community. Large- and medium-sized parishes are as likely to have a strong sense of community as are small parishes. Furthermore, the parishes of town and countryside are *less* likely to have a strong sense of community, while the parishes of city and suburb are *more* likely—just the opposite of the usual expectation. Finally, we found little relationship between whether a parish was theologically conservative or progressive and the sense of community; even in the theologically conservative parishes, the parishioners expect greater lay responsibility.

## Conclusion

When we review all our data about leadership and parish context, we return to the conclusion that each parish makes its own destiny. Each parish has indigenous potential leaders; shy though they be about volunteering, they are waiting to be asked and affirmed. Each parish, because of the mobility of American Catholics, will have a trickle or a flood of people who were leaders in another parish; the new parish must learn how to welcome their ideas and service. Each parish can pay staff to serve them, but the pool of funds will be larger in those parishes that avoid a new "staff clericalism" or hyperprofessionalism and enlist parishioners in volunteer cadres alongside the staff. And each parish will respond to the charisms of the pastor assigned to it for a spell; some parishioners will reject their pastors, and the ordination of baptism will fail to surface; others will embrace him and will share in every way the responsibilities of parish life. Sometimes parishioners will have sufficient self-confidence about their ministries that they can survive one or two bad assignments. The larger suburban, city, and some town parishes are better positioned to do so than other parishes of town and countryside, which, lacking organizational complexity, cannot insulate pastor and people from direct contact for long.

Our *Report* series has offered vignettes, little stories of leadership in each parish (Leege, 1986b; 1987). From them the lesson is clear: if parish leadership is a plural noun, there is still no component more important than the vision and skills of the pastor. For it is the pastor who calls and cajoles the laity to responsibility, who affirms or dismisses their huge or humble efforts. Each parish has a particular story. The pastor must learn the important symbols in that story, must allow himself to be schooled by the parishioners. For when he can accommodate to their cultural identity, he can offer a vision that will mobilize them toward his objectives.

## NOTES

1. This chapter is based on the Notre Dame Study of Catholic Parish Life, an examination of a probability sample of nearly eleven hundred parishes in 1982, and an intensive study of thirty-six representative parishes during 1983–84. The findings have been presented in scholarly papers but are especially accessible in the fifteen-part *Report* series edited by David C. Leege and Msgr. Joseph Gremillion from 1984 to 1989 (Leege and Gremillion, 1984). This paper draws not only on data from the eleven hundred parishes, but uses questionnaires addressed to pastors, the "most influential" paid staff and volunteer leaders, and probability samples of parishioners within each of the thirty-six parishes, and on parish histories, ethnographies, observations, and semistructured interviews. The author is indebted to the study's funder, the Lilly Endowment; to Robert Lynn, Msgr. John Egan, and the Rev. Philip Murnion, who collaborated in the initiation of the project; to Fred Hofheinz, and Profs. Michael Welch, Jay Dolan, and Mark Searle, who helped to see the research through; and to Msgr. Joseph Gremillion and two assistants, Thomas Trozzolo and Edwin Hernandez, who played important roles in the *Report* series.

## WORKS CITED

Burkart, Gary P., and David C. Leege
      1988      "Parish Life in Town and Countryside." *Notre Dame Study of Catholic Parish Life*, Report 13. University of Notre Dame.

Conrad, Ann Patrick, and Joseph J. Shields
      1982      "Career Lay Ministers in the Archdiocese of Baltimore: An Assessment of Future Roles and Functions." Washington, D.C.: Center for Applied Research on the Apostolate.

Dolan, Jay P.
      1985      *The American Catholic Experience: A History from Colonial Times to the Present.* Garden City, N.Y.: Doubleday & Co.
      1989      "American Catholics in a Changing Society: Parish and Ministry, 1930 to Present." In Jay P. Dolan, R. Scott Appleby, Patricia Byrne, and Debra Campbell, *Transforming Parish Ministry: The Changing Roles of Catholic Clergy, Laity, and Women Religious.* New York: Crossroad.

Dolan, Jay P., and David C. Leege
      1985      "A Profile of American Catholic Parishes and Parishioners: 1820s to the 1980s." *Notre Dame Study of Catholic Parish Life*, Report 2. University of Notre Dame.

Fox, Zenobia V.
    1986        "A Post–Vatican II Phenomenon: Lay Ministries: A Three-
                Dimensional Study." Ph.D. Dissertation, Fordham University.

Greeley, Andrew M.
    1985        *American Catholics Since the Council.* Chicago: Thomas More
                Press.

Hemrick, Eugene F., and Dean R. Hoge
    1985        *Seminarians in Theology: A National Profile.* Washington,
                D.C.: U.S. Catholic Conference.

Hoge, Dean R.
    1987        *The Future of Catholic Leadership: Responses to the Priest
                Shortage.* Kansas City, Mo.: Sheed & Ward.

Hoge, Dean R., Raymond H. Potvin, and Kathleen M. Ferry
    1984        *Research on Men's Vocations to the Priesthood and the Reli-
                gious Life.* Washington, D.C.: U.S. Catholic Conference.

Leege, David C.
    1986a       "Parish Organizations: People's Needs, Parish Services and
                Leadership." *Notre Dame Study of Catholic Parish Life,* Re-
                port 8. University of Notre Dame.
    1986b       "Parish Life Among the Leaders." *Notre Dame Study of Cath-
                olic Parish Life,* Report 9. University of Notre Dame.
    1987        "The Parish as Community." *Notre Dame Study of Catholic
                Parish Life,* Report 10. University of Notre Dame.

Leege, David C., and Joseph Gremillion
    1984        "The U.S. Parish Twenty Years After Vatican II: An Introduc-
                tion to the Study." *Notre Dame Study of Catholic Parish Life,*
                Report 1. University of Notre Dame.
    1986        "The People, Their Pastors, and the Church: Viewpoints on
                Church Policies and Positions." *Notre Dame Study of Catholic
                Parish Life,* Report 7. University of Notre Dame.

Leege, David C., and Thomas A. Trozzolo
    1985        "Participation in Catholic Parish Life: Religious Rites and Par-
                ish Activities in the 1980s." *Notre Dame Study of Catholic
                Parish Life,* Report 3. University of Notre Dame.

Schoenherr, Richard A., and Annamette Sorensen
    1982        "Social Change in Religious Organizations: Consequences of
                Clergy Decline in the U.S. Catholic Church." *Sociological
                Analysis* 43 (Spring): 23–52.

Walters, Thomas P.
    1983        *National Profile of Professional Religious Education Coor-
                dinators/Directors.* Washington, D.C.: National Conference of
                Diocesan Directors of Religious Education.

Westoff, Charles F.
    1979        "The Blending of Catholic Reproductive Behavior." In Robert
                Wuthnow, ed., *The Religious Dimension,* 231–240. New York:
                Academic Press.

# THREE

# Hymn-Singing:
# The Congregation Making Faith

## LINDA J. CLARK

In answer to a question about why she picked a particular hymn as her favorite, a woman responded, "It sounds the way following Christ is like!" This statement expresses in very few words the relationship between hymn-singing and faith. To this woman, her favorite hymn provides a living symbol of what a life of faith feels like. Singing it among her friends in her local church on a Sunday morning enlivens her faith because she *tells* it in the singing. Hymns and other aesthetic forms found in worship are carriers of faith, and congregations create hymns in order to manifest their faith in the world.

This essay provides a detailed explanation of the experience described in the woman's characterization of her favorite hymn. Its primary focus is the congregation that gathers on a Sunday to worship together; and, although most of the essay concerns hymn-singing, the principles that are set forth can be applied to other aesthetic forms in worship—ritual acts, preaching, architecture—including the event of worship itself.

For the sake of conciseness I will speak from my experience as a Protestant. Hymns occupy a position of importance in Protestant worship that they do not in other traditions. However, other religious traditions are not bereft of aesthetic forms. Roman Catholics will find similarities in what follows. The music and rituals of the Mass are similar carriers of the faith of the congregation. The silent Quakers, although not a singing community, sit in certain patterns, in buildings that are beautiful in their simplicity and grace.

In the course of this essay I will describe what I mean when I use the terms "tradition" and "hymn," and then show how such an ordinary, "homegrown" form becomes a statement of faith and why usually mild-mannered folk who inhabit Christian communities can become outrageously loud and outspoken when members of hymnal committees begin to meddle with their hymnbooks! Finally, an extended illustration using a hymn of Isaac Watts will show how the forms themselves are shaped by communities who sing them—how in "making faith," hymns can be changed around and their meanings transformed by the people who need them.

## Tradition Defined

There are many ways to describe religious traditions. For purposes of this essay I want to describe a religious tradition as an uninterrupted string of moments or events connected through the telling of stories. These stories, told by people as a way of making sense out of their lives, are learned or written down, to be told or read aloud amid others who like themselves are searching for meaning. Public worship is one place where these stories about the human condition are transmitted from one generation to another. Worship can be characterized as a congregational form of storytelling. Through worship what is of ultimate value in the past of a community is brought into the present and enlivened. Aesthetic forms by their very nature allow new meaning to arise with each "rehearsal." Each time a story is told, something new is created out of the experiences that it evokes. Through this process of new creation the present is transformed.

These moments of transformation are moments of hope because they provide a way to enter the future creatively. Having told the stories that link the valued past of their community with the present, the congregation is released into the uncertain future firmly rooted in its identity. Stories *have* plots and characters but their basic and pervasive structure *is* hope. Thus not only do the plots and personages of these stories preserve that which is of ultimate value to a community, the very act of telling also functions that way.

A form of storytelling found in most worship is hymn-singing. Many hymn texts are actually little stories. One that immediately comes to mind is "Where Cross the Crowded Ways of Life." However, hymns are stories in a broader sense too, because the singing of them declares something very important about the people who sing them. Hymns *are* stories and *have* stories; they often bring events from the past with them in the singing. There are remnants of the past stuck to certain hymns; these "stuck pasts" transform and anchor the present, joining it to other dimensions—more primitive, more numinous, more *affective*.

## Hymns Defined and Described

Hymns are the Protestant equivalent of the Orthodox icons and therefore serve both expressive and formative functions in a person's faith. Hymns provide the means through which people express their faith, and when people sing hymns their faith is formed by the experience. What kind of "icon" is a hymn? Obviously we do not hang hymns on a wall and look at them as we would the icons that come from the traditions of Eastern Orthodoxy. No. *A hymn is a highly complex set of images, both verbal and aural, set in motion through singing by a group of people who have intentionally gathered to worship God.* Each word and phrase in that sentence is important, and I will explain each phrase in turn, illustrating what I say by referring to the pilot project "Music in Churches," a study of music programs in churches sponsored by the Boston University School of Theology and funded by the Lilly Endowment. The proper use of hymns and the vitality of congregational hymn-singing were objects of great comment in all segments of the project.

### Hymns as Sets of Images

The images of a particular hymn, both poetic and musical, initially draw the worshiper into the world of a hymn. "Rock of Ages," "Love Divine, All Loves Excelling," "A Fountain Filled with Blood," "In the Garden," the "walking bass" in "For All the Saints," the ascending melodic line that accompanies the text "Up from the Grave He Arose," the particular harmonic cast to "Let All Mortal Flesh Keep Silence"—these images evoke a kind of fascination in worshipers that draws them into the world of the hymn and holds them there while the meaning is clarified through experience. Avery Dulles, in *Models of the Church*, speaks of the way images "mean" in the religious sphere:

> In the religious sphere, images function as symbols. That is to say, they speak to man existentially and find an echo in the inarticulate depths of his psyche. Such images communicate through their evocative power. They convey a latent meaning that is apprehended in a nonconceptual, even a subliminal, way. Symbols transform the horizons of man's life, integrate his perception of reality, alter his scale of values, reorient his loyalties, attachments, and aspirations in a manner far exceeding the powers of conceptual thought (1974:18).

As Dulles points out, images are evocative and convey *latent* meaning. They take on the energy of fascination, which then "sticks" to the subsequent events to which they are linked by the imagination. Hymn images accompany the singers throughout their lives and surface in ordinary places, often without bidding, to reinterpret experience.

For me, the last lines of Charles Wesley's "Love Divine, All Loves Excelling" have that kind of power.

> Changed from glory into glory,
> Till in heaven we take our place,
> Till we cast our crowns before thee,
> Lost in wonder, love, and praise.

I cannot remember when I first noticed them (here the slang expression "They grabbed me!" is highly appropriate) but for a long time now they have had a kind of fascination attached to them. The hymn has a numinous quality to it. "It sounds the way following Christ is like!" That numinosity functions to educate me in faith when it erupts from the psychic depths to confront me. It helps to mitigate the terror of my own death, for it shows that something in my soul knows that death involves not only terror but also the experience of wonder, love, and praise of God. In the midst of my daily round, I find myself occasionally singing those lines and I ask myself, "Why have I suddenly started singing those lines of Wesley's?" Hearing of a friend's courage in the face of serious illness, risking my own comfort and safety to help someone in need, noticing the beauty of fall in New England—events like these touch another, less ordinary layer of my existence and evoke the images of that hymn.

### Hymns as Images Set in Motion

Singing puts the words of a hymn into motion. Hymns are not static sets of words on a page but shapes of sound that exist in time, beginning at one moment, traveling toward a point, and then drawing to a close and stopping at another moment. This shaping of time heightens the meaning of texts. The philosopher Susanne Langer explains why. In trying to describe how music has meaning, she states, "What music can actually reflect is . . . the morphology of feeling. . . . [It] conveys general forms of feeling" (1957:238). In other words, music is an aural image of the shape of feeling alive. "It is not self-expression, but formulation and representation of emotions, moods, mental tensions and resolutions—a 'logical picture' of sentient, responsive life, a source of insight" (1957:222). When members of a congregation sing together, the words of the hymn come alive to them and mean more than just a statement of fact. In hymn-singing they are pouring out their own hearts. The hymn creates that faith by bringing it into being and therefore is functioning as a symbol of the singers' faith. As Dulles explains:

> The symbolic expression does not simply signify what previously existed independently of it. Rather, the expression and the realization accompany and support each other. The corporeal expression gives the spiritual act the material support it needs in order to achieve itself; and the spiritual act gives shape and meaning to the corporeal expression (1974:61).

A hymn does not only *tell of* the faith, it *tells* it, declares it, or bodies it forth.

Hymn-singing often takes on a quality similar to a sacrament and other rites of the church. It becomes what Dulles would call "an efficacious sign":

> [A] sign . . . produces or intensifies that of which it is a sign. Thanks to the sign, the reality signified achieves an existential depth; it emerges into solid, tangible existence. Because of the incarnational structure of the human spirit, every reality of the spiritual order necessarily seeks to achieve its proper form of expression, and then lives off the expression it achieves (1974:61).

Using Dulles's language, a hymn produces or intensifies the faith that its images carry or evoke. As a community sings "Were You There When They Crucified My Lord?" it journeys back to that hillside so vividly captured in the Christian imagination and relives the faith that that image has carried throughout the ages. Yet it is important to point out that what the journey back to that hillside retrieves is *not* the actual experience of the crucifixion itself. If the actual crucifixion were relived, there could be no singing. No, it is an image of the crucifixion that comes alive. It is a metaphor for the *faith* born of the contemplation of the crucifixion. As such the singing of the hymn can serve to transform any tragic event by reminding the singers of that faith and connecting them to it in the depth of their suffering. Even by standing mute in the midst of people singing the hymn, persons can have their suffering transformed as the community becomes their voice when their own fails them.

To illustrate this point, here is a woman speaking of her favorite hymn:

> [It] recalls Christ's very human pain with simple, sad reverence. It is quiet and contemplative and reminiscent of my most memorable conversion experience.

Here is her description of her conversion experience:

> [It] was on Good Friday, 1983. I was living in ——— and was fairly heavily involved in a church there. I sang in the adult choir, a commitment I took very seriously. I was praying during the last few minutes of the three-hour service when at once I was overcome by the presence of Jesus and His suffering, death and resurrection. I suddenly knew that I was forgiven; that I was loved; that Jesus had been there and was here now for me. I started to sob uncontrollably and wept for some time. That day was a major turning point in my relationship with God.

This woman relates the experience her favorite hymn carries for her. A significant moment in her past is brought into the present and she reaffirms her faith in its singing.

### Hymns as Communal Events

The faith that is produced by hymn-singing is reinforced by the communal event in which the individual is caught up. A singer does not simply contemplate the images of the hymn in solitude, but stands amid others and sings as one among many. The potential for transformation is magnified because one sings in a group; the group itself adds elements of chance and change that might not be as prevalent in isolation or solitude. One enters a realm where one is not alone; the ordinary psychic boundaries are transcended and energy is permitted to flow back and forth among the group, in and out. The feeling of this movement is highly pleasurable. Moreover, the sheer sound of a group singing lends the hymn power.

One woman confessed when asked about hymn-singing in worship: "[I] would like to try to sing harmony on my favorite hymn—'Dear Lord and Father of Mankind'—at least once a month!" She spoke of the joy of adding a part to the concerted praise of the congregation. In other interviews people came up with ways to saturate the community with music, getting everyone involved in all sorts and levels of music-making from concerts to additional worship services, expanding the choir, making the congregation more like a choir, redesigning the church to give the congregational singing more verve and body. "I want this group to sing with more gusto!" In such a communal state one is more vulnerable, less in control, and therefore can sense the interdependence that signifies communal life at its most profound.

Many people remarked on the sense of history the music in worship brought to them: "Surrounded by a cloud of witnesses," one person said of the composers that weekly were brought to life through the choir anthems. Not only are the boundaries between individuals transcended, the boundaries of time are also transcended as the past merges with the present. Moreover, the particular past that is brought into the present through hymn-singing is often one marked by heightened awareness and the potentiality for transformation: memories of a funeral of a beloved aunt, a crisis in the community, one's marriage or ordination. Expressive forms carry "a *qualitative* dimension of the historical experience" (Meland, 1987:118; emphasis added) into the present. A hymn brings the felt experience that has coagulated around its images (musical and poetic) into the room at each rendition. This "past/present" experience of faith usually happens at a very primary psychic level—on the boundary of conceptual thought, touching the mystery of existence itself.

## Hymns Used in Worship

The intention by which a particular community undertakes to do something lends meaning to the experience. Worship is no casual gathering but one set aside for prayer and praise in communion with God and one's neighbors. Things undertaken under such circumstances take on a force that might not be there under other circumstances. Hymn-singing in church on Sunday derives meaning from the intent of the gathered community to worship God. The hymns themselves play various roles in worship. A service of worship is itself a very complex art form which, like music, has a beginning, middle, and end. Worship is shaped time, and hymns often help to shape it. For example, hymns at the end of worship often have a "sending-out" character. The existence of suspended motion and concentrated energy in the fifty-five minutes preceding the singing of the final hymn help give it a quality that the opening hymn will not have had.

The above-mentioned characteristics of the event that is "hymn-singing" serve to intensify and lend a special quality to it. Hymns function as other religious symbols do. Recall the words of Avery Dulles, quoted above: "Symbols transform the horizons of man's life, integrate his perception of reality, alter his scale of values, reorient his loyalties, attachments, and aspirations in a manner far exceeding the powers of conceptual thought" (1974:18). Furthermore this particular set of symbols—the hymn—accomplishes that task in the midst of a community and thus binds that community into one.

Hymns both express and form faith. A hymn is an object, made up of sound existing in time, which one sings as a way of expressing one's faith.

As one sings it, one's faith is formed, because in the act of expressing one's faith in symbolic forms, something new comes into existence. The cultural anthropologist Clifford Geertz writes:

> The central connection between art and collective life does not lie on . . . an instrumental plane, it lies on a semiotic one. . . . [It] material-ize[s] a way of experiencing; bring[s] a particular cast of mind out into the world of objects, where [people] can look at it (1976:1478).

The favorite hymns of a person or a community are not "about" the faith of the people; they *are* their faith. And as Dulles points out, "Every reality of the spiritual order necessarily seeks to achieve its proper form of expres-sion, and then lives off the expression it achieves" (1974:64). Thus on Sunday morning people "make" faith as they stand to sing hymns in the congregation of the faithful.

## Aesthetic Objects and the "Mythos" of a Community

It is clear from the above description of the aesthetic object we call a hymn that congregational hymn-singing is a powerful act, but in what ways does it carry a religious tradition? There are hints about this issue in the foregoing description: hymns have pasts and carry the past into the pres-ent. The tradition and the past of a community are closely intertwined, and hymn-singing often brings that past to life. However, the subject needs more than just hints to explain it, and therefore I turn now to a more detailed and systematic explanation of the relationship between a religious tradition and an aesthetic object such as a hymn.

### "Mythos" Defined

According to the theologian Bernard Meland, expressive forms, such as stories, myths, and other imaginative constructs, grow out of or reflect a community's mythos:

> By mythos I mean something more than a particular mode of reflective-ness or poetry. The mythos encompasses these responses, but it includes them along with other more visceral and imaginative assertions of the psychical thrust of a people. . . . [It] shap[es] the sensibilities, apprehen-sions, expectations, intentions, and valuations of a people. . . . The no-tion of mythos partakes of the stream of experience as well as of the stream of thought. And it gathers in as well inert, though symbolically significant, precedents and practices which body forth . . . the *inten-tionality* of a people (1976:113).

"Mythos" encompasses and fashions the expressive forms that *tell* the identity of a community and of its faith. These forms are myths and stories, images and symbols, events and rituals. Meland is speaking here of a level of experience, often subconscious, that precedes and supports what we would recognize as ordinary experience—the sensibilities that declare what is of value, what is cherished, what is intended of a community. In worship, the daily habits of thought and being are suspended momentarily as a community enters the realm of the mythic. Through prayer and praise congregation members proclaim their faith in forms that, because they express the qualities of their identity that are often disguised or unexpressed or exist prior to "normal" reality, partake of the extraordinary and the numinous. Without these forms the community dries up, stagnates.

A community's myths, stories, rituals carry forward the "qualitative dimension of the historical experience"; they present through symbol and metaphor those aspects of experience that are indirect, emotional, laden with meaning. They *body forth* the tradition; the verb "body forth" is very important as a way to describe how *material* and how *embodied* this act of transmittal of the history of a people is. Mythos incorporates that aspect of the tradition which expresses and informs the ethos of a people—what it values and cherishes and what motivates it. It is expressive of the *intentionality* of a community.

James Hopewell, in his book *Congregation*, describes the power of the mythos of a congregation when he tells of the disastrous fate of his seminary course on ministry in the church he calls Trinity. There he stumbled into a hornet's nest because he was ignorant of one of the controlling myths of its congregation. The church's myth, unspoken yet very much alive, bodied forth the values and intentions of the people of that congregation. Hopewell's course ran at cross-purposes to the very thing that made that church live. Attention to their stories and the myth that lay behind them would have relieved him of such a disaster, as he himself points out in the book.

The favorite hymns of a congregation are also an expression of the mythos of the people who comprise it. As anyone who has worked in the church for longer than six months can tell, the favorite hymns are ignored to the peril of the leadership of any congregation. If they are, a hue and cry is inevitable because these events bring to life aspects of the tradition *which only live through them*. Nothing can take the place of singing these hymns. The "funded sensibility" that is a hymn is communal, emotional, and expressive of the highest values of the singer. Surely any community that neglects such sensibility has a limited future (as well as a sterile one).

In the project many men who had served in World War II chose the "Navy Hymn" as their favorite ("Eternal Father, Strong to Save"). That hymn represented for them one of the most profoundly human times in their pasts as well as one in which their faith was tested to an extreme. What singing that hymn does for them now is to recall that time *in all its emotional vividness*. Communities are strengthened and blessed when times such as these live again among them.

### Aesthetic Objects Fashioned by Mythos

In the foregoing pages I have been discussing how an icon or expressive form like a hymn carries aspects of a religious tradition, particularly the mythos of communities, into the present. At this point I would like to illustrate another way this process might occur by showing how congregations change hymns—make them over to express their ongoing faith experience. In this instance one sees how a community modifies forms to fit its needs to body forth its own values and intentions. I will examine what happens to a text, this one from the pen of Isaac Watts, when it comes into use in a different religious tradition and how the modified text portrays the sensibilities of a people far removed from the time and place of the original author.

The text I have chosen to investigate is a famous one: "Alas! and Did My Saviour Bleed!" It appeared in Watts's first book of hymns, *Hymns and Spiritual Songs*, published in London in 1707. Here is the text as Watts wrote it:

> Alas! and did my Saviour bleed!
> And did my Sov'reign die;
> Would he devote that sacred head
> For such a worm as I!
>
> Thy body slain, sweet Jesus, thine,
> And bath'd with its own blood,
> While all expos'd to wrath divine
> The glorious sufferer stood!
>
> Was it for crimes that I had done,
> He groaned upon the tree?
> Amazing pity! Grace unknown!
> And love beyond degree.

> Well might the sun in darkness hide,
> And shut his glories in,
> When God the mighty Maker dy'd
> For man the creature's sin.
>
> Thus might I hide my blushing face,
> While his dear cross appears,
> Dissolve my heart in thankfulness,
> And melt my eyes to tears.
>
> But drops of grief can ne'er repay
> The debt of love I owe:
> Here, Lord, I give myself away;
> 'Tis all that I can do.

The caption that Watts appended to this text was "Godly sorrow arising from the suffering of Christ." Like many hymns, it has a strategy: It presents a dilemma as it describes the figures in the text—God, Jesus, and the singer—and then presents a "strategy" for its solution. In this case, the singer repays the debt owed to God by giving himself or herself away.

This text, missing its second stanza, appears in the new *United Methodist Hymnal* (1989) with a very important addition—a chorus:

> At the cross, at the cross,
> Where I first saw the light,
> And the burden of my heart rolled away,
> It was there by faith
> I received my sight,
> And now I am happy all the day!

Where did the chorus come from? Who added it? Why? The answers to these questions tell a story about communities at worship—a story about their faith: what was of value to them, what they cherished, what their intentions were.

Watts's text appeared in thousands of publications in America, including many that provided hymns for the revivals taking place along the frontier in the early nineteenth century. These hymns were altered frequently in the heat of religious fervor. George Pullen Jackson, a chronicler of the folk music of early America, furnishes three different versions of the text with three different tunes in his collection, *Spiritual Folk-Songs of Early America* (1964:221, 226, 240). All three of them show the influence of their use at camp meetings as a means to bring about conversion. In practice people used bits and pieces of these hymns over and over again, working themselves and others through the various stages of the conversion process. Through repetition and call and response they simplified the hymn and made it more dramatic.

Here is a description of the opening of a camp meeting in which the use of music is chronicled:

> The opening service was held on the first night, usually Thursday. Following the assembly of participants in the seats in front of the stand, the service began when a preacher started a spiritual song which was picked up by the congregation. There was usually no sermon in this service, nor in any night service; rather it was an alternation of ministerial exhortations and congregational singing. The alternation continued until mourners began to enter the pen, at which time the singing became a constant accompaniment to the exhortations and invitations of the preachers. At some point the power of God came down, causing singers to fall and more mourners to approach the altar, often with the aid of ministers and church members. The physical exercises, begun in the seating area, now centered in the pen. As soon as enough mourners had come forward, the ministers left the pulpit and moved into the pen themselves where they continued to exhort and invite and to counsel individual mourners. Good singers and praying persons also entered the pen, where they surrounded the fallen to give encouragement and comfort (Bruce, 1974:80f.).

The chorus in the last hymn portrays the actual emotional experience of conversion—the yielding to God amid an intense internal struggle against sin and the devil. Here is one John Hagerty writing to a friend about his conversion:

> It was not long before the Lord shewed me the remains of sin that was left within which caused many doubts and fears and made my soul to mourn for a deliverance from them. . . . That Scripture was often imprest on my mind "Without holiness no man shall see the Lord." I knew I was far from it for I saw so many things in me contrary to the will of God that I was afraid I should at last fall away. On Monday my distress was deepened and on Tuesday I thought my heart would break for it appeared as if all the powers of hell were engaged against me. I never knew before as I did then what it was to be tempted. On Wednesday I thought I could believe the Lord would deliver me. I went to class meeting and soon after we begun my Brother broke out in praising God which greatly encreased my distress. It was imprest on my mind to kneel down and pray. I resisted it but it returned the second time. I thought if I did not it would

be the last time that the Lord would strive with me which caused me to cry mightily to the Lord for deliverance. I was in a short time enabled to lay hold on Jesus Christ and found salvation by simple faith. I believe He removed my sins as far from me as the east is from the west. I do not know if I have felt anything contrary to love since. . . . My soul is happy this moment, and I believe I shall be like Him, for when He shall appear I shall see Him as He is (Sweet, 1946:127f.).

The particular chorus that appears in the new *United Methodist Hymnal* originally appeared in another famous revival hymnal, this one the product of the urban revivals that followed the Civil War. *Gospel Hymns, Nos. 1 to 6 Complete,* published in Chicago by Biglow and Main in 1894 and edited by Ira D. Sankey, the musician connected with evangelist Dwight Moody, contains a truncated version of the Watts text with the appended chorus. One can almost hear John Hagerty singing it. Such procedures favored easily grasped, easily remembered verse and refrain forms of hymnody. Often the refrains that were attached to the verses of a hymn consisted of fragments from the original text. Another practice was to detach a chorus from one hymn and attach it to another in the heat of the moment. Here are the texts that Jackson collected.

### Come Friends Go with Me

Alas! and did my Savior bleed,
Alas! and did my Savior bleed,
Alas! and did my Savior bleed
And did my Sov'reign die?
Would He devote that sacred head
For such a worm as I?

Chorus:
I want my friends to go with me,
I want my friends to go with me,
I want my friends to go with me
To the new Jerusalem.
I wonder, Lord, shall I ever get to heaven?
The new Jerusalem.

### Victoria, or One More River to Cross

Alas! and did my Savior bleed,
Alas! and did my Savior bleed,
Alas! and did my Savior bleed
And did my Sov'reign die?

Chorus:          I have but one more river to cross,
                 I have but one more river to cross,
                 I have but one more river to cross,
                 And then I'll be at rest.

### I Yield

Alas! and did my Savior bleed,
And did my Sov'reign die?
Would He devote that sacred head
For such a worm as I?

Chorus:          I yield, I yield, I yield,
                 I can hold out no more;
                 I sink by dying love compell'd,
                 And own thee conqueror.

Alas! and did my Savior bleed!
And did my Sov'reign die;
Would He devote that sacred head
For such a worm as I!

Chorus:          At the cross, at the cross,
                 Where I first saw the light,
                 And the burden of my heart rolled away,
                 It was there by faith
                 I received my sight,
                 And now I am happy all the day!

Was it for crimes that I have done,
He groaned upon the tree?
Amazing pity, grace unknown,
And love beyond degree.

Chorus:          At the cross, at the cross . . .

But drops of grief can ne'er repay
The debt of love I owe:
Here, Lord, I give myself away;
'Tis all that I can do.

The hymn is called "At the Cross" and has the following caption, from Isa. 45:22: "Look unto me, and be ye saved" (1894, no. 305). The chorus radically changes the dignified and solemn statement by Watts into a rollicking testimony of faith. Watts, who found the revivals of his day led by such luminaries as George Whitefield and the Wesley brothers too excessive, probably rolled over in his grave when Moody and Sankey cranked up this hymn! The camp meeting, where the hymns of both Watts and Charles Wesley were very popular, molded many a text to the values and intentions of the conversion experience. Some of them were "amicable" changes; others were gross distortions. Hymns, more easily than any other aesthetic form, become the property of the people who sing them and therefore are more readily influenced by the community's character and history.

## Conclusion

Aesthetic forms carry religious traditions by expressing the mythos of communities. On Sunday mornings in congregations across the land people "make" faith through the singing of hymns. Malleable and charged with affect, hymns provide the means for the great truths of a religious tradition to come alive to each generation and to be reinterpreted and changed by the experience of each generation. As Geertz points out, art is a manifestation of a way of experiencing; hymn-singing is a manifestation of the faith of the people who comprise a religious tradition and who form that religious tradition. To the woman whom we quoted at the outset, her favorite hymn sounded the way *her life* felt when she followed Christ. Even though she did not write the hymn, she made it her own every time she stood up in the assembly and sang it. The people in the clearing in the midst of a revival *did* write their own hymns by piecing together fragments of texts and choruses from other hymns that everyone knew. They took what was "lying around" to make a form whose emotional power would help themselves and others through the struggle with sin. By doing so they created a body of song that tells the story of their faith.

Herein lies the basis for hope, for the very structure of aesthetic forms provides for their reappropriation by people of every generation. If the hymns were lost, the tradition would die. If the hymns became so rigid that they lost the capacity to interpret the lives of hearers in every generation, the tradition would die too. Because the hymns are made to live, week in and week out, the tradition lives and the people of the tradition lay hold on the hope they need to live out their faith in the world that surrounds them.

## WORKS CITED

Bruce, Dickson
    1974       *And They All Sang Hallelujah.* Knoxville: University of Tennessee Press.

Dulles, Avery
    1974       *Models of the Church.* Garden City, N.Y.: Doubleday & Co.

Geertz, Clifford
    1976       "Art as a Cultural System." *Modern Language Notes* 91.

Hopewell, James F.
    1987       *Congregation: Stories and Structures.* Edited by Barbara G. Wheeler. Philadelphia: Fortress Press.

Jackson, George Pullen, ed.
    1964       *Spiritual Folk-Songs of Early America.* New York: Dover Publications.

Langer, Susanne K.
    1957       *Philosophy in a New Key.* Cambridge, Mass.: Harvard University Press.

Meland, Bernard
    1976       *Fallible Forms and Symbols.* Philadelphia: Fortress Press.
    1987       "Myth as a Mode of Awareness and Intelligibility." *American Journal of Theology and Philosophy* 8 (September).

Sweet, William Warren
    1947       *Religion on the American Frontier: 1783–1840.* Vol. 4: *The Methodists.* Chicago: University of Chicago Press.

# FOUR

# The Black Church and Social Ministry in Politics and Economics: Historical and Contemporary Perspectives

## C. ERIC LINCOLN AND LAWRENCE H. MAMIYA

From their beginnings, independent black churches have attempted to minister to the spiritual, physical, and social needs of their congregations and communities. The proscriptions of two hundred and fifty years of slavery followed by another one hundred years of segregation in both the South and the North allowed only the church to become a stable, cohesive, and independent black social institution. An important result of this historical process meant that black churches have had to assume collateral roles and burdens in areas other than specifically religious ones in morality, politics, economics, education, music, and culture (Frazier, 1974). Nevertheless, in spite of their unchallenged significance in the maintenance of black communities, black churches are often stereotyped as inordinately obsessed with otherworldly concerns, as an "opiate" of the masses, rather than with the practical matters of here and now (Marx, 1969; Reed, 1986).

Much of this stereotype is fostered by the intense emotional involvement common to most black worship services. It is rooted in a misunderstanding of the relationship between the religious dimension of black worship and the social ministry, which begins with the worship occasion and finds its ultimate expression in community service. This chapter will examine some expressions of the social ministries of black churches in the areas of economics and politics in the late nineteenth century (Reconstruction to the twentieth century), and in the contemporary period (the civil rights period to 1988), which may be helpful in demythologizing the "opiate" stereotype of the Black Church.[1] These historical and contemporary examples of black social ministries may also provide useful models of community involvement for all churches and clergy to consider. The narrative descriptions and findings in this chapter are drawn from a national study of black churches, "The Black Church in the African-American Experience," which was funded by the Lilly Endowment.

## The Social Ministry of Black Churches During Reconstruction to the Twentieth Century: The Political and Economic Spheres

Prior to the Civil War, free blacks and African slaves learned to shape the emerging fusion of African, European, and American cultural elements into a religious instrument for their own survival and liberation. Indeed, this African-American Christianity ultimately prevented the complete dehumanization of the slaves (Genovese, 1974). The "invisible institution" or underground church of slave religion, which was often practiced secretly without the presence of whites, merged with legitimate black Baptist and Methodist churches from the mid- to late eighteenth century (Frazier, 1974). From 1619, when twenty Africans were brought to the Jamestown colony by a Dutch slave ship, until 1865, the major focus of black political activity was the slave system. In the South, black slaves used any possible means to get away from the onus of slavery; they ran away, plotted uprisings, and sometimes were able to purchase their freedom. If all else failed, they even committed suicide.

The notion that slavery was inconsistent with the will and the character of God was subliminal to all slave religion; thus the three largest slave revolts in American history were planned and led by slave preachers: Gabriel Prosser in 1800 near Richmond, Virginia; Denmark Vesey in 1822 in Charleston, South Carolina; and Nat Turner in 1831 in Southhampton County, Virginia (Wilmore, 1983:53–63). In the North, the abolitionist movement pressed for the eradication of the slave system. The homes of white abolitionists and black churches became "stations" for hundreds of escaped slaves on the underground railroad to northern cities and to Canada. For example, the basement of the Mother Bethel A.M.E. Church in Philadelphia was used by Bishop Richard Allen to hide escaped slaves, and numerous other black church leaders and their congregants risked their lives to further the cause of freedom. The A.M.E. Zion Church became the spiritual home for some of the most legendary figures of the abolitionist movement, including Frederick Douglass, Sojourner Truth, Harriet Tubman, the Rev. Jermain Louguen, Catherine Harris, Eliza Ann Gardner, and the Rev. Thomas James (Wilmore, 1983:87).

The emancipation of close to four million slaves at the end of the Civil War brought enormous challenges to black churches and to the nation. A devastated southern economy and the hostility of their impoverished former owners meant that there were few resources to house, feed, and care

for these destitute former slaves. In most instances the freedmen were left
to fend for themselves, since neither the Union armies nor the missionaries
who often accompanied them were equipped to handle the enormous problem. While some of the more enterprising freedmen migrated to Oklahoma
and Kansas, the majority stayed in the South and gradually formed black
communities in rural towns or near their former plantations. These first
black communities, as W. E. B. Du Bois observed, were usually formed
around their churches, since they were the first communal institutions and
the initial matrix of "economic cooperation among Negroes" (Du Bois,
1907:54).

The first economic undertakings of black churches were lessons in
household finances, teaching former slaves how to handle money, and most
important, instructions in economic rationality, of saving for a rainy day
and the virtues of delayed gratification. Black churches had the formidable
job of restoring the damage done by the slave system to black families by
emphasizing the infinite worth of every human personality in God's eyes,
and by encouraging black men to assume the responsibility previously
denied them as the heads of families. Perhaps the most important contribution of black churches to the process of black economic survival was their
stress upon acquiring an education and their establishment of black educational institutions, often in the churches themselves. Classic examples include Morehouse College, which began in the basement of the Springfield
Baptist Church in Augusta, Georgia. The origins of Spelman College can be
traced to the Friendship Baptist Church in Atlanta. Tuskegee Institute was
founded in the basement of the Butler Chapel A.M.E. Zion Church in
Tuskegee, Alabama. In many black communities, the first rudimentary
lessons of reading and writing were given in Sunday school to both children
and adults. The importance of religion to the education of the former slaves
is shown by the fact that thousands of them, old and young, crammed every
school set up by northern missionaries or the black churches. Although
many of the freed men and women realized that this education would not
get them jobs in a war-torn economy, they knew that it would enable them
to read the Bible for themselves.

Black churches often spawned allied institutions such as mutual aid
societies, quasi-religious fraternal lodges like the Masons and the Elks, and
benevolent and burial associations. These organizations were often responsible for the creation of the first black financial institutions such as the
banks and life insurance companies. However, it was only after the collapse
of the government-sponsored Freedman's Savings and Trust Company in

1874 that black-owned financial institutions became symbolic of the determination of the emergent black community to develop its own financial
base (Blassingame, 1973:67). Chartered by Congress in 1865, the Freedman's Savings and Trust Company was the major bank that held most of
the savings of the newly emancipated African Americans, the bounties that
black soldiers received upon enlisting in the Union army, and the deposits
of numerous philanthropic organizations, benevolent associations, and
churches. Its collapse, brought on by the national recession of 1873 and
aided by the incompetence of bank officials, caused widespread financial
distress and distrust among many African Americans toward banks. This
distrust still lingers in the conventions that shape the attitudes of the black
poor about saving money and about the reliability of financial institutions
(Blassingame, 1973:67–68).

In 1887 there was not a single black-owned bank but within two decades,
by 1908, fifty-five banks had been started and forty-seven were in operation
(Coles, 1975:105–106). The fraternal lodges and churches helped to capital-
ize Negro banks such as the True Reformers' Bank in Richmond, Virginia,
and the Capital Savings Bank of Washington, D.C., both founded in 1888.
While the fraternal orders were the primary mobilizers of black finance, the
churches ranked second and black pastors often played a prominent role in
organizing insurance societies and banks (Coles, 1975:105–106). As Meier
and Rudwick observed, "The True Reformers' Bank, the Galilean Fisher-
men's Bank, and the St. Luke's Bank were all either founded by ministers or
closely connected with the churches" (1970:196). The historical museum in
the basement of the Sixteenth Street Baptist Church in Birmingham, Alabama, also contained mementoes of the Penny Saver Bank, established at the
church for its members in the late nineteenth century. The bank's first
president was the pastor.[2]

Toward the end of the nineteenth and at the beginning of the twentieth
century, the first Negro insurance companies began to appear, growing
from the financial resources of both the mutual aid and burial societies in
many churches and the fraternal orders. In examining the origins of one of
the largest Negro life insurance companies, North Carolina Mutual, Meier
and Rudwick discerned the following pattern:

> In the life of John Merrick, the man chiefly responsible for North Caro-
> lina Mutual, one of the largest black life insurance companies, one ob-
> serves the evolution of Negro insurance from the quasi-religious
> fraternity society through the chartered mutual-aid organization to the
> legal reserve company (1970:197–198).

Merrick founded North Carolina Mutual in 1898, while Alonzo Herndon established the rival Atlanta Life Insurance Company in 1905. The Afro-American Industrial Insurance Society of Jacksonville, Florida, was established in 1902 from a mutual benefit society in a black Baptist church.

The practice of segregated cemeteries in the North and the South and the difficulties of obtaining loans from white lending agencies led to the establishment of black cemetery associations and building and loan institutions. The first building and loan association in Philadelphia was founded in 1886, and in twenty years there were ten such institutions, most of which resulted from the organizational skills of the black clergy (Meier and Rudwick, 1970:196).

In the political sphere African Americans were able to participate in electoral politics for a brief period of time during the Reconstruction period beginning in 1867. But this participation was severely curtailed after Rutherford B. Hayes's infamous southern compromise of 1877, which removed federal troops from the South in exchange for southern electoral votes in a deadlocked presidential contest. However, during their brief time of effective franchise thousands of former slaves registered to vote and they succeeded in electing twenty black congressmen and two black senators. In 1870 an A.M.E. clergyman, the Rev. Hiram Revels of Mississippi, became the first black citizen and the first black senator elected to Congress. The Rev. Richard H. Cain served four years in the state senate and two years in the U.S. House of Representatives; he became a bishop in the A.M.E. Church in 1880. Numerous other black clergy served in elective or appointive political positions at the local level. The influence of the Black Church was such that various factions sought to influence the black vote through its leadership on the theory that the church functioned substantially as a political organization. John Van Dusen writes:

> The most effective method (of controlling the black vote) was to bribe the preachers, since the Negro church was a kind of political organization and those who voted contrary to the direction of their spiritual guides were ostracized and sometimes expelled from the church (Van Dusen, 1936).

The most radical political voice in the last decades of the nineteenth century was Bishop Henry McNeal Turner of the A.M.E. Church. As an organizer for the Republican party, Turner helped to build a black political base in Georgia. As a theologian, he raised a considerable controversy through his black nationalist liberation theology, which began with the premise that "God Is A Negro." Turner was the singular voice among black clergy calling for reparations for slave labor. He also supported the emigration movement, which advocated the resettlement of African Americans in Africa (Turner, 1898; Wilmore, 1983).

The removal of the protection provided by federal troops, unrestrained Ku Klux Klan violence, economic discrimination, an ever-increasing number of restrictive black codes, and electoral obstacles such as poll taxes and frivolous registration procedures finally led to a virtually complete disenfranchisement of black voters in the South by the end of the nineteenth century. Jim Crow segregation was ratified and legitimated by the highest court in the land through the doctrine of "separate but equal" laid down in the *Plessy v. Ferguson* decision of 1896. Thereafter, for close to a hundred years, from the failure of Reconstruction until the passage of the Voting Rights Act of 1965, the Black Church became the main arena for black political activity. Excluded from the mainstream electoral process, black people voted and chose their leaders in their churches, selecting pastors, bishops, trustees, deacons and deaconesses, presidents of conventions and women's auxiliaries, and the like. This surrogate politics carried on in the Black Church became an intensive training ground of political experience with all the triumphs and disappointments of which the political process is capable. It was the one area of social life where leadership skills and talents could be honed and tested, and it was the only area for most blacks where the struggle for power and leadership could be satisfied.

Black Church leadership at its highest levels has always presumed a political astuteness unique to the calling. Management and leadership of a large black congregation presupposed, first of all, the exclusion of a segregated society and the concomitant authority and responsibility derived from the people who were affected by that segregation. Hence, the black church leader of consequence must have extraordinary bureaucratic and leadership skills as well as political ability. The opportunity to develop these skills was necessarily restricted to involvement in church leadership, but they were skills that could easily be transferred outside the church should the opportunity ever present itself. Fund-raising, public speaking, organization and mobilization, campaign strategy, and administration were skills that retained their viability in almost any sphere of human enterprise.

The Black Church had significant political meaning for the future of electoral politics in the black community, providing experience in democratic polity, political evaluation, and the exercise of the right and the responsibility to vote. These experiences enabled African Americans to make an easier transition to mainstream political participation after the most obstructive barriers to civil rights had been removed.

## The Black Church, Urban Migrations, and the Civil Rights Movement

According to the 1890 census, the first to give an urban-rural breakdown, nine out of ten black people then lived in the South and about 80 percent of them resided in the rural counties commonly called "the Black Belt" (U.S. Department of Commerce, 1980). In 1980 about 85 percent of the black population lived in urban areas and only about 53 percent lived in the South (Johnson and Campbell, 1981). The vast migrations from the rural South to the urban North and West were clustered around the periods of World Wars I and II and the Korean War. They transformed the American landscape as millions of black people left the Black Belt in search of jobs and a better life.

The effects of the great urban migrations upon black churches were twofold. First, rural churches in the South sustained a considerable loss in membership and clergy, resulting in seriously reduced church activity and leadership (Richardson, 1947). Second, while the established urban churches often doubled or tripled their membership as a result of the migrations, other migrants and their pastors established numerous smaller churches in rented storefronts. Many black sects and cults also had their beginnings in the chaos of the urban migrations as new spiritual leaders such as Marcus Garvey, Father Divine, and Elijah Muhammad arose to challenge the dominance of the Black Church.

The political responses of black clergy and churches varied during the period of the migrations. Some progressive clergy were instrumental in helping to establish civil rights groups like the National Association for the Advancement of Colored People and the National Urban League; in fact, both groups found their primary support in black church congregations. However, the Depression of 1929 profoundly affected the political and economic activities of black churches. The Depression brought failure to all the black banks the churches had helped to create; only the larger insurance companies such as North Carolina Mutual, Atlanta Life, and the Afro-American Insurance Society survived. It also brought to a halt most of the economic experiments that black churches had initiated or supported. Nevertheless, many black churches continued to be involved in local urban

politics during the interwar years, primarily as mobilizers of the black vote
in cities like Chicago, where blacks became important clients of "Big Bill"
Thompson's Republican political machine (Gosnell, 1935). But the large
numbers of unlettered rural migrants, and the devastating economic conditions that gripped black communities, pushed many other black churches
into a conservative political stance, and many of the new storefront
churches withdrew into a revivalistic sectarianism. Wilmore has characterized this interwar period as the "deradicalization of the Black Church"
(Wilmore, 1983: ch. 6). But while few black churches exhibited the characteristics of a militant black nationalism such as Marcus Garvey's United
Improvement Association or Elijah Muhammad's Nation of Islam, they
were not necessarily "depoliticized." Many black churches continued to
play a role in mobilizing black voters and providing a forum where political
candidates could address the members of the black community. Other issues of interest to black people were similarly put forward through the
agency of the churches. A. Philip Randolph's fledgling black labor union,
the Brotherhood of Sleeping Car Porters, for example, used the black local
churches as a primary organizational base for recruitment and financial
support (Peeks, 1971:285).

While many black church leaders courted low visibility by taking a
nonconfrontational, behind-the-scenes approach toward civil rights and
economic issues, a few clergy like the Rev. Adam Clayton Powell, Jr., of
the Abyssinian Baptist Church in Harlem adopted more radical strategies
such as civil rights protests in the streets on economic issues in the late
1930s. Using his eight-thousand-member Abyssinian Baptist Church as his
base, Powell organized the Greater New York Coordinating Committee,
which helped him to get elected to the U.S. House of Representatives in
1944, the first black politician from the East to serve in Congress (Powell,
1945:95–103). He eventually became the chairman of the House Committee on Labor and Education, making him the most powerful black politician since Reconstruction. An effective if controversial preacher-politician,
Adam Clayton Powell made major legislative contributions that helped
pave the way for the rise of the civil rights movement.

If the interwar years were a relatively quietistic time for black church
leadership, with such notable exceptions as Powell, the civil rights period
ushered in by *Brown v. Board of Education* in 1954 was a period of
extensive turmoil and violence. It was also a time of intense black politici-
zation. Ironically, the first area of American society to be desegregated was
the U.S. Army under orders from President Harry Truman in compliance

with the Civil Rights Act of 1947. The next target was public schools and education. The case that came to symbolize a decisive break with the past began when Rev. Oliver Leon Brown of the St. Mark A.M.E. Church in Topeka, Kansas, supported by the NAACP Legal Defense Fund, sued the board of education on behalf of his nine-year-old daughter Lynda Brown and all other black children similarly injured by segregation in the public schools. The resultant Supreme Court decision granting the relief requested set in motion the civil rights movement, which reached its zenith under the leadership of the Rev. Dr. Martin Luther King, Jr., with reverberations around the world. It was Dr. King who led the year-long Montgomery bus boycott, which began in December 1955 and which culminated in a decisive defeat of segregation in the public transportation system of that onetime capital of the Confederacy. While King provided the public leadership, it was the black church women of the Women's Political Council in Montgomery who provided the crucial network of organization and support. Two years later King organized the Southern Christian Leadership Conference as the political arm of the Black Church. SCLC gave decisive focus and direction to local church involvement in the civil rights movement, and hundreds of black clergy and their congregations made extraordinary sacrifices to move the cause forward.

Black churches were the major points of mobilization for mass meetings and demonstrations, and black church members fed and housed the civil rights workers from SNCC, CORE, and other religious and secular groups. Most of the local black people, who provided the bodies for the demonstrations, were members of black churches acting out of convictions that were religiously inspired. Black church culture also permeated the movement from oratory to music, from the rituals and symbols of protest to the ethic of nonviolence (Morris, 1984). It is estimated that several hundred churches in the South were bombed, burned, or attacked during the civil rights years, with ninety-three such incidents occurring between 1962 and 1965, more than fifty in Mississippi alone. The white opposition understood their importance (Hilton, 1969:182).

The civil rights movement is a major watershed in the annals of Black Church history and the history of the nation, and the role of the Black Church in whatever success that movement has accomplished is self-documented. Martin Luther King emerged from the civil rights tumult as the symbolic and mythic figure of that era. The movement has not been completed, and the crusaders have not yet "overcome." Before his death, King and other civil rights leaders were involved in organizing a Poor

People's Campaign to march on Washington, D.C., because they realized that true freedom presupposes freedom from want. The next phase of the movement was the need to focus on economic issues and economic inequality. Having the civil right to sit in a restaurant if one could not afford to eat there proved to be a hollow victory indeed, so the new black political strategy was to use political power via protest and electoral politics as a lever for economic access and opportunity.

## The Social Ministry of Black Churches in the Contemporary Period: The Political and Economic Spheres

*Black Preacher-Politicians and the Role of Black Churches in Electoral Politics*

In the 1980s, probably no other political phenomenon drew as much attention or stirred as much controversy as the candidacy of the Rev. Jesse L. Jackson in the 1984 and 1988 presidential campaigns. Jackson was unusual on two counts: he was black and he was a preacher-politician. The American commonwealth enshrined the doctrine of the separation of church and state in its founding document, and that principle has had an inhibiting effect on clergy with aspirations for political office. Nonetheless, the preacher-politician is not unknown to American history. Among whites recent examples include Massachusetts' Father Robert Drinan, who was elected to the House of Representatives, and the Rev. Pat Robertson, who campaigned for the Republican presidential nomination in 1988. For African Americans, preachers were always among the prime community leaders and the phenomenon of preacher-politician was as routinely accepted as it was pervasive. Senator Hiram Revels, an A.M.E. clergyman, set the pattern of elected black preacher-politicians in the Reconstruction period.

Besides Jesse Jackson, the most notable black preacher-politicians in the twentieth century include Adam Clayton Powell, Jr.; Andrew Young, former mayor of Atlanta and former ambassador to the United Nations; William E. Gray III, who chaired the powerful Budget and Finance Committee of the House and recently became the chairperson of the House Democratic Caucus; Walter Fauntroy, delegate to Congress from the District of Columbia; and John Lewis, representative of the Fifth Congressional District in Atlanta, Georgia. In the fall of 1986 this select group of preacher-politicians was joined by the Rev. Floyd H. Flake, pastor of the Allen A.M.E. Church in Queens, New York, who was elected to the House of Representatives from the Sixth Congressional District of New York City.

Flake's political investiture followed the classic pattern set by Adam Powell.

After leaving his position as university chaplain and dean of students at Boston University, Flake was appointed in 1976 by his bishop to the pastorate of the Allen A.M.E. Church in Jamaica, Queens, a respectable working-class church with fourteen hundred members and a $250,000 annual budget. Over the next decade he promoted a neighborhood revitalization program, establishing church-based corporations that worked with city agencies to rehabilitate local stores and homes. Under his leadership, the church built an $11 million senior citizen housing complex, including a senior citizen center. He also completed the $3.8 million Allen Christian School and Multi-Purpose Center attached to his church. The school has an enrollment of four hundred eighty students from the kindergarten to the eighth grade. The church also sponsored a home care agency in cooperation with the City of New York to provide home attendants for those who require such help, and there is a health center to provide clinical, pregnancy, postnatal, and other services (May, 1987). Allen A.M.E. Church presently has five thousand members, eight subsidiary corporations with a thousand employees, and a yearly budget of $12 million.

Flake's first involvement with electoral politics was as a Jesse Jackson delegate to the 1984 Democratic convention, and as a leader of a black voter registration effort. After the sudden death of Representative Joseph F. Addabbo in 1986, Flake was encouraged to run for the vacated post by a group of local black clergy, who promised the support of the religious community. After an initial setback in his attempt, Flake eventually won the 1986 Democratic primary by defeating the Democratic machine's black candidate Aldon Waldron, and he easily won the general election.

The Rev. Floyd Flake's election to the U.S. House of Representatives provides several important lessons as a case study, especially in illustrating the significant role of black churches as the potential bases for political mobilization. Voluntary associations are vital to American electoral politics, and in black communities the churches are the dominant voluntary associations of consequence. Other ethnic groups such as the Irish, Italians, and Jews have also used their churches and synagogues for political mobilization with telling effect (Stabrowski, 1985). Second, Flake's story indicates the need to broaden our view of politics beyond the confines of "electoral politics" and to include the kinds of community organizing and empowering activities long common to black churches. Feeding and housing destitute people, tending to their physical, psychological, and spiritual needs, providing dignity and status, are ultimately ways of being political. As the *Amsterdam News* reported about Flake's victory, people saw how he made a difference in transforming the church and the community with the limited resources available to him and "they felt that as Congressman, he could use the same model to change Southeast Queens" (Anekwe, 1986:1). Third, political success is not automatic for the clergy. The work of community organizing and caring for people must come first. Examples such as Adam Clayton Powell, Jr., William Gray, and Floyd Flake underscore the lesson: they all began by working on people's problems first. As Flake commented, "The church is not just a building, it is a community. The people are the church" (Hazel, 1985:11).

The vocation of preacher-politician is a difficult prophetic task, fraught with many problems and complexities. Not every preacher is qualified for public office and those who undertake it are subject to all the conflicts, pressures, temptations, compromises, and corruption of political life. Furthermore, the task of attempting to do two full-time jobs leads to the strain and frustration of doing neither well. However, the political process is present in contemporary life and it has to be guided and used responsibly. For black churches and clergy to withdraw from the political sphere because it is tainted would be the ultimate act of irresponsibility to the concerns and needs of an oppressed and disempowered people. The task of the prophet in the ancient world or in the modern world has always involved "dirty hands" on behalf of a mission from the Creator; to pronounce the word of judgment and to be judged at the same time. Prophecy has always been a double-edged sword. The history of the social ministry of the Black Church has legitimated the role of the preacher-politician and the role of black congregations in politics.

It is important to recognize that black clergy have never been the sole leaders of black communities; there have always been leaders, such as Frederick Douglass, Booker T. Washington, W. E. B. Du Bois, Sojourner Truth, and Mary McLeod Bethune, who have been nonclerical, but they were usually members of black churches. Since the 1960s, two sources of secular black leadership have developed to challenge the traditional dominance of the clergy: grassroots community leaders who were trained in the community action programs of the War on Poverty, and professional black politicians who have begun to use their offices as sources of patronage (Preston, Henderson, and Puryear, 1982). However, while the leadership platform is usually shared by black clergy and secular political leaders, black church congregations are still critical as important sources of political mobilization.

*The Black Church and Black Economic Development*

As mentioned above, the economic experiments of black churches were severely hampered by the fatalities of the Depression. While there have been notable exceptions, recovery has been slow and halting. In his *Social Teaching of the Black Churches*, Peter Paris observed that black churches never gave "high institutional priority to black economic development," but they put their energy instead into "education, moral training, and civil rights" because they saw these areas as "necessary conditions for economic development" (Paris, 1985:69–70). However, since the end of the civil rights period in 1968, the area of black economic development has become a more pressing concern, and there is evidence that some black churches, mostly the large institutional urban black churches with highly educated pastors, have become involved again with economic issues and problems. The sociological data over the past twenty years have shown that the "crisis sector" of the black poor, with all of its attendant problems, has grown from 25 percent in 1968 to over 33.1 percent nearly twenty years later (Wilson, 1987). At the same time there has been an increase in the "coping sector" of middle-income black people, made up of the black middle and working classes (Landry, 1987). However, the effects of institutional racism have resulted in very high levels of residential segregation for African Americans, and black-owned businesses have remained a stunted 2 percent of all businesses since 1970 (Williams, 1986:181). In this section, we will present a brief case study of the significant leadership role of the Rev. Leon Sullivan of Philadelphia in the area of black economic development and give a summary of the kinds of economic development projects that some black churches have undertaken in the 1980s.

The Rev. Leon Sullivan, pastor of the Zion Baptist Church of Philadelphia, has provided the leadership for some of the most important economic development projects involving black churches since the civil rights period: the Progress Investments Associates and the Opportunities Industrialization Centers. Educated at Union Theological Seminary in New York City and apprenticed to the Rev. Adam Clayton Powell, Jr., at the Abyssinian Baptist Church, Sullivan organized the "Selective Patronage Campaign" in the late 1950s in Philadelphia, which was supported by four hundred black ministers. The campaign successfully boycotted such corporate giants as the Tasty Baking Company, Sun Oil, Atlantic-Richfield, and Pepsi-Cola. This success led to requests from employers for skills in technical fields, which many blacks did not possess at that time, because of racial exclusion. Sullivan then recognized the need for a community-based employment

training facility, which was founded in 1964 as the Opportunities Industrialization Centers of America (Stone, 1986:8).

Another economic development project that also paved the way for OIC
was Sullivan's "10-36" plan initiated in his church in 1962. The plan
called for church members to voluntarily contribute $10 for 36 months to
support the Philadelphia Investment Cooperative. The group of two hundred twenty-seven original subscribers grew to over five thousand with
about four hundred black churches participating, and $200 of every $360
subscription was invested in a for-profit corporation called Progress Investments Associates, Inc. The remaining $160 was donated to the Zion
Non-Profit Charitable Trust. The Progress Investments Associates built the
Progress Plaza Shopping Center, the first and largest black-owned and
operated shopping complex in the United States. It also constructed an
apartment building, a garment manufacturing plant, and a chain of convenience stores. Zion Non-Profit Charitable Trust used foundation and
government grants to sponsor programs such as housing for the disadvantaged, remedial education, and other human services activities (Stone,
1986:13). Through these projects, Sullivan was replicating the historical
role that the Black Church and its clergy played in economic development
and giving it the new directions the times demanded. Indeed, one of Sullivan's economic development tutors was the famous Father Divine, who had
earlier moved his headquarters to Philadelphia from Harlem when Sullivan
began his ministry at the Zion Baptist Church. Father Divine was the black
economic genius of the Depression, feeding and housing thousands of people in New York, Philadelphia, and elsewhere when even the federal government did not prove equal to the task (Weisbrot, 1983). Divine's method
of economic cooperation among poor people as a means of self-help and
economic uplift fascinated Sullivan.

When it was formed in 1964, the Opportunities Industrialization Centers of America quickly became a nationwide phenomenon, operating in
seventy cities within five years and handling federal government contracts
worth $18 million (Stone, 1986:9). A distinctive feature of the OIC ap-
proach has been the development of a close working relationship with the
private sector, which facilitates job placement activities and generates corporate contributions (Stewart, 1986:23). Another distinctive feature of
OIC job training programs involves the attempt to stimulate a moral commitment from the trainees and to inspire feelings of self-worth through
classes on black history. This spiritual and moral dimension of OIC distin-
guishes it from federal Manpower and other job training programs.

The expansion of OIC has depended primarily upon the support of local ministers and churches in various communities, a pattern that is consistent with its origins. Although OIC does not have any formal ties with churches, four of the top five officers of the OIC National Board of Directors are ministers. Opportunities Industrialization Centers, Inc., represents one of the more successful job training programs initiated by black church leadership. Projects like OIC show that Rev. Sullivan has been an example par excellence of the modern black minister involved in the complexities of economic development issues by leading and teaching his and other black congregations to participate in self-help and cooperative projects.

A growing number of large black urban churches have also revived the tradition of church involvement in businesses and economic development of their communities. Under the leadership of the Rev. Dr. Gardner Taylor, America's largest black church, the Concord Baptist Church (with an estimated fifteen thousand members) in the Bedford-Stuyvesant section of Brooklyn, has established a nursing home, a private elementary school through the eighth grade, a clothing bank, and a credit union, and has two full-time social workers on its staff. Another Brooklyn church, the four-thousand member Bethany Baptist Church, pastored by the Rev. William A. Jones, has raised $1 million to open the Harvest Manor Restaurant, which employs forty-four people (Gaither, 1983). The Rev. Floyd Flake's Allen A.M.E. Church in Jamaica, Queens, has set up a church-sponsored housing corporation that rehabilitated ten stores in the neighborhood. The church also has a housing development fund, a home care agency, a three-hundred-unit, $11 million complex for senior citizens, and a four-hundred-eighty-pupil elementary school. And the Abyssinian Baptist Church in Harlem, inspired by the Rev. Dr. Calvin Butts's community involvement, has built four housing complexes for poor people.

Other examples of large black churches involved in economic development projects include St. John Baptist Church in Miami, Florida; Allen Temple Baptist Church in Oakland, California; Hartford Avenue Baptist Church in Detroit; New Zion Baptist Church in Louisville, Kentucky; and Antioch Baptist Church in Chicago's Southside (*Ebony*, 1987:62–64). In the largest housing cooperative project of its kind in the nation, fifty-five East Brooklyn churches have undertaken to build five thousand owner-occupied row houses within ten years, called the Nehemiah Houses in honor of the prophet of the fifth century B.C. who rebuilt Jerusalem. Forty percent of the owners will come from public housing projects, and a thousand units have already been built.[3]

In Atlanta, the Wheat Street Baptist Church is probably the wealthiest black church in the country, infusing the surrounding community with more than $15 million worth of development. The church also owns a middle-class apartment building, Wheat Street Towers, and it is landlord to a number of storefronts along Auburn Avenue in the black business district. Beyond that, Wheat Street is reputed to own some twenty acres of downtown Atlanta. Wheat Street is pastored by the legendary Rev. William Holmes Borders, who set up the first federal credit union sponsored by any church and is considered one of the pioneers in church-sponsored public housing.

Recent research suggests that most of the economic development sponsored by the Black Church is undertaken by large congregations with well-educated leadership and a predominantly middle-class membership. For the smaller and less sophisticated churches, the dearth of financial awareness and expertise, and the traditional priority given spiritual concerns in such churches, still substantially inhibits the activism that economic development implies. Hence, while impressive, the examples cited must, for the time being at least, be recognized as exceptions to the prevailing state of the Black Church. But there is definitely an emergent propensity toward increased economic awareness, which could in time reinforce substantially the social effectiveness of the Black Church as the counterpart of its traditional political commitment.

Denominational polity appears to be an important factor in regard to the sponsorship of economic development projects by black churches. In our field survey, we observed that more than 90 percent of the black churches involved in economic projects were the elite black Baptist churches in urban areas with relatively little challenge from Methodist or Pentecostal institutions. The independent congregational polity of the Baptists, where each congregation and pastor is autonomous in major decisions, tends to be more conducive to an independent entrepreneurial spirit. The more centralized "connectional" church polity of the Methodists, with a system of bishops, a central church fund, church taxes, and the principle of itinerancy, which requires relocating pastors every few years, tends to inhibit this entrepreneurial spirit. The length of time that a black pastor remains in a particular community is often crucial to community confidence and commitment, as well as to the priorities of his leadership decisions.

In terms of theology, it has been noted that many black church members generally have a conservative evangelical theological stance but they also tend to support liberal social justice ministries in economics and politics. In contrast, the study of white affluent churches by Davidson, Mock, and Johnson described in chapter 4 of this book indicates that white churches that are active in social justice ministries tend to have a liberal theological stance. The difference between black and white churches probably has less to do with theological orientation than with the concreteness of social location and felt racial oppression. On the whole, because they are victims of oppression, black Christians with either liberal or conservative theological views have generally supported ameliorative social programs. The seven historic black denominations have always held to an anti-racial discrimination stance.

Black churches also have a strong historical tradition of being pastor-centered institutions, with the black pastor having a greater range of authority than most white clergy. Hence, much of the social activism of black congregations in economics or politics usually requires the consent and leadership of the pastor. This tradition of strong authority by the pastor arose at a time when the clergy were usually considered among the best educated leaders in the black community, but its deeper roots are in the biblical patriarchal tradition. At times this high level of authority invested in the office of the pastor may take on autocratic proportions (Frazier, 1974:90). However, with the rising levels of education and the creation of a stable black middle class, greater emphasis will be placed upon the democratic processes of lay participation in decision-making. Lay leadership in future social outreach ministries will become a more critical factor of determination than tradition has allowed.

## Conclusion

Born of slavery and racism, the Black Church has been both a spiritual refuge to heal the pain of an outcast people and an instrument of liberation. The social conscience of the Black Church has been more overt and more pronounced at some times and places than at others. While this unevenness has exasperated those who have a one-dimensional perspective on the Black Church, its inherent genius is that it recognizes human beings as both spirit and body with a duality of needs that must be addressed, and that both are constantly at risk in American society. However, the record is clear that the Black Church and its leaders have been active with varying degrees of effectiveness in both the political and economic spheres throughout the history of its existence. Some black clergy have been willing to take on the additional responsibilities of public office and involvement in the political arena as forms of their social ministry. Other clergy and churches have used their imaginative and financial resources to create economic institutions needed by their people: banks, insurance companies, building and loan associations, federal credit unions, apartment buildings, and housing complexes, including the largest black-owned shopping plaza complex and one of the largest job-training programs in the United States.

A historical overview of the social ministries of black churches indicates their uniqueness in being more active over a broad range of economic and political concerns than most churches in the United States. However, this uniqueness should not preclude other clergy, church leaders, and laity from learning about the significant models of social ministry found in the history of black churches. Above all, black churches have been fairly successful in challenging the effects of modernity on the church, particularly the tendency to separate religion from the public sphere and to withdraw into a sphere of private piety. The social ministry of the Black Church has been undergirded by a continuity of holistic theological perspectives that its ministry, caring for and serving people, ought to encompass all of life, including not only the spiritual but also the political and economic dimensions as well.

## NOTES

1. The coauthors of this chapter are the principal investigator and the associate principal investigator, respectively, of the national study "The Black Church in the African-American Experience." The term "Black Church" is operationally defined as referring to the seven major historic black denominations: the National Baptist Convention, U.S.A., Inc.; the National Baptist Convention of America; the Progressive National Baptist Convention, Inc.; the African Methodist Episcopal Church; the African Methodist Episcopal Zion Church; the Christian Methodist Episcopal Church; and The Church of God in Christ.

2. Notes of field visit to the Sixteenth Street Baptist Church in Birmingham by Lawrence Mamiya in May 1979. This church was bombed in 1963, during the civil rights movement, and four young girls attending Sunday school were killed.

3. This coalition of East Brooklyn churches also includes predominantly black congregations from white denominations such as the Catholics and the Lutherans.

## WORKS CITED

Anekwe, Simon
        1986          "Flake, Vann, and Green Win Over Challengers." *The Amsterdam News*, November 8, p. 1.

Blassingame, John
1973    *Black New Orleans, 1860–1880.* Chicago: University of Chicago Press.

Coles, Flournoy A., Jr.
1975    *Black Economic Development.* Chicago: Nelson-Hall Co.

Du Bois, W. E. B.
1907    *Economic Cooperation Among Negroes.* Atlanta: Atlanta University.

*Ebony* Staff
1987    "Church Businesses Spread the Gospel of Self-Help." *Ebony* 42 (February): 61–64.

Frazier, E. Franklin, and C. Eric Lincoln
1974    *The Negro Church in America;* and *The Black Church Since Frazier.* New York: Schocken Books.

Gaither, Dorothy
1983    "Church Opens a Restaurant in Brooklyn." *The New York Times,* April 23, p. B3.

Genovese, Eugene
1974    *Roll, Jordan, Roll: The World the Slaves Made.* New York: Random House.

Gosnell, Harold
1935    *Negro Politicians: The Rise of Negro Politics in Chicago.* Chicago: University of Chicago Press.

Hazel, Brenda Huger
1985    "Gospel Balance . . . It's Happening in Jamaica, New York." *The Cornerstone* (Allen A.M.E. Church, Jamaica, N.Y.; edited by Anqunett Fusilier, published by James Fanner), pp. 10–12.

Hilton, Bruce
1969    *The Delta Ministry.* New York: Macmillan Co.

Johnson, Daniel M., and Rex R. Campbell
1981    *Black Migration in America: A Social Demographic History.* Durham, N.C.: Duke University Press.

Landry, Bart
1987    "The New Black Middle Class (Part II)." *Focus* (Washington, D.C.: Joint Center for Political Studies) 15/10 (October).

Levine, Lawrence
1978    *Black Culture and Black Consciousness.* New York and London: Oxford University Press.

Marx, Gary
1969    *Protest and Prejudice.* Revised edition. New York: Harper & Row.

May, Clifford D.
1987    "Queens Congressman Balances Duties in Church and the Capitol." *The New York Times,* March 30, pp. B-1, B-5.

Meier, August, and Elliot Rudwick
    1970        *From Plantation to Ghetto.* Rev. ed. New York: Hill & Wang.

Morris, Aldon D.
    1984        *The Origins of the Civil Rights Movement.* New York: Free
                Press.

Paris, Peter J.
    1985        *The Social Teaching of the Black Churches.* Philadelphia: For-
                tress Press.

Peeks, Edward
    1971        *The Long Struggle for Black Power.* New York: Charles
                Scribner's Sons.

Powell, Adam Clayton, Jr.
    1945        *Marching Blacks: An Interpretive History of the Rise of the
                Black Common Man.* New York: Dial Press.

Preston, Michael B., Lenneal J. Henderson, and Paul L. Puryear, editors.
    1982        *The New Black Politics: The Search for Political Power.* New
                York: Longman.

Reed, Adolph L.
    1986        *The Jesse Jackson Phenomenon.* New Haven and London: Yale
                University Press.

Richardson, Harry V. B.
    1947        *Dark Glory: A Picture of the Church Among Negroes in the
                Rural South.* New York: Friendship Press.

Stabrowski, Donald J.
    1985        "A Political Machine, an Ethnic Community, and Leadership's
                Use and Acceptance of Incentives: A Case Study of South
                Bend's West Side: 1909–1979." Ph.D. dissertation, University
                of Notre Dame.

Stewart, James B.
    1986        "The Black Church as a Religio-Economic Institution." Pre-
                pared as a background paper for the national research project
                "The Black Church in the Black Experience," under the aus-
                pices of Lincoln and Mamiya, Department of Religion, Duke
                University.

Stone, Sonja H.
    1986        "The Opportunities Industrialization Centers as a Religio-
                Economic Institution." Prepared as a background paper for
                the national research project "The Black Church in the Black
                Experience," under the auspices of Lincoln and Mamiya, De-
                partment of Religion, Duke University.

Turner, Henry McNeal
    1898        "God Is A Negro." *Voice of Missions* (African Methodist Epis-
                copal Church), February, p. 1.

U.S. Department of Commerce, Bureau of the Census
 1980  *The Social and Economic Status of the Black Population in the United States: An Historical View, 1790–1978.* Current Population Reports, Special Studies Series P. 23, no. 80. Washington, D.C.: U.S. Government Printing Office.

Van Dusen, John G.
 1936  "The Negro in Politics." *Journal of Negro History* 21 (July).

Weisbrot, Robert
 1983  *Father Divine and the Struggle for Racial Equality.* Champaign, Ill.: University of Illinois Press.

Williams, James D., ed.
 1986  *The State of Black America 1986.* New York: National Urban League.

Wilmore, Gayraud
 1983  *Black Religion and Black Radicalism.* 2nd ed. Maryknoll, N.Y.: Orbis Books.

Wilson, William Julius
 1987  *The Truly Disadvantaged: The Inner City, the Underclass and Public Policy.* Chicago: University of Chicago Press.

# FIVE

# Threading the Needle:
# Faith and Works in Affluent Churches
## ALAN K. MOCK, JAMES D. DAVIDSON, AND
## C. LINCOLN JOHNSON

The congregation as a corporate body is called to carry out many tasks—to take on numerous roles. To the church, nurturing deep trust in God is one of the most important tasks of the church. The church is to reveal to its members and the world the compassion and mercy of God's love, to teach the redemption of sin through Jesus' crucifixion, and thus to be thankful and praise God. "Let the word of Christ dwell in you richly, teach and admonish one another in all wisdom, and sing psalms and hymns and spiritual songs with thankfulness in your hearts to God" (Col. 3:16). Nurturing faith in God and Jesus Christ is simply at the heart of what the church is about.

Yet the church and its members are called to other tasks as well: "If a brother or sister is ill-clad and in lack of daily food, and one of you says to them, 'Go in peace, be warmed and filled,' without giving them the things needed for the body, what does it profit? So faith by itself, if it has no works, is dead" (James 2:15–17). Being faithful thus seems to mean helping those in need, putting others before self, and striving for justice. If churches are to nurture the faith of members and be faithful themselves, they simply cannot ignore the injustices of hunger, poverty, and war. Churches must not only actively spread the Good News among members and the unchurched, they must serve the needs of the disadvantaged and advocate the rights of the oppressed.

These two tasks are no small tasks indeed, and they seem particularly problematic for affluent churches—churches with a disproportionate number of fairly wealthy members working in highly paid, prestigious business and professional occupations.

Common wisdom holds that affluence does not easily share a close kinship with a deep faith in God, nor with an active concern for the disadvantaged. The well-to-do, it is thought, would rather spend their time playing

golf or relaxing at their summer homes than worshiping on Sunday, praying, or participating in a Sunday school class discussion. They look to
money, position, and power for comfort and security rather than to a faith
in the love of God. Programs and activities within the church that go much
beyond a token effort of nurturing such belief and trust are thought to be
looked upon with disdain by the affluent.

Conventional wisdom also holds that the affluent are not particularly
concerned about hunger, poverty, and racial inequality. It is thought that
the rich believe that they have earned—and thus deserve—their privileged
place in the world and that the poor—because of inferior abilities and
motivation—essentially deserve to be poor. According to this image, affluent church members do not believe their churches should be involved in
social reform programs that seek to redistribute wealth and power, or in
"giveaway" programs that foster dependency and thwart initiative among
the poor. Thus, most people expect little from affluent churches in nurturing faith or promoting justice.

Even the Bible notes the difficulty of maintaining deep faith and concern for others when money and power get in the way. "Again I tell you, it
is easier for a camel to go through the eye of a needle than for someone who
is rich to enter the kingdom of God" (Matt. 19:24, NRSV). The rich presumably cannot enter heaven because of their reluctance to do two things:
to fully trust God rather than wealth and power, and to seek greater justice
and equality in society.

Many scholars have found support in their data for this image of affluent
churches. Max Weber (1964:107) observed that, "other things being equal,
classes with high social and economic privilege will scarcely be prone to
evolve the idea of salvation. Rather, they assign to religion the primary
function of legitimizing their own life pattern and situation in the world."
Liston Pope (1942:92), in his study of the church and labor movements of
the 1920s, noted that the "greater economic security . . . [of] 'uptown' "
churchgoers in Gastonia, North Carolina, fostered an attitude that "religion must not meddle too much in private life. . . . For uptown people,
religion—well, it's just religion—which is to say, it is a set of actionways
and thoughtways associated with, and largely confined to, the church." To
the extent that affluent churches played any public role, they were "to a
considerable degree a sanction of prevailing economic arrangements."
Gibson Winter (1962:206–207) called attention to the "deterioration of
public worship and public responsibility" among suburban Protestant
churches during the 1950s. He explored what he termed the "spiritual

emptiness," the "communal exclusiveness," and the "introversion" of
these affluent churches. More recently, Birch and Rasmussen (1978:46)
said that America's affluent churches have "given a materially self-
indulgent way of life one benediction upon another."

But interestingly, many recent writers have observed a number of affluent churches that do not fit the prevailing image. Thomas Sweetser (1983)
has shown that some affluent Catholic parishes are communities of intense
faith. B. Carlisle Driggers's (1979) collection of congregational life histories
includes several relatively well-to-do Protestant churches that have been
actively engaged in the social and economic concerns of their communities.
Hadden and Longino's book *Gideon's Gang* (1974) described the formation and activities of an affluent congregation in Dayton, Ohio, that became
actively involved in quite radical forms of social ministry. Donald Smith
(1981) explored a number of Presbyterian churches that were quite successful in nurturing faith and promoting justice. James Davidson (1985)
noted that some affluent churches were highly involved in the formation
and success of an ecumenical urban ministry that seeks to serve and advocate the rights of the disadvantaged. The various styles of religious presence identified by Roozen, McKinney, and Carroll (1984)—such as
"civic" and "activist"—included affluent churches.

## The Dilemma

We are thus confronted with a bit of a dilemma: Just what are affluent
churches like? Do wealth and power among church members discourage
the nurture of pious and righteous faith? Or can the affluent church inspire
intense faith among its members? Do the privileged positions of their members thwart the involvement of affluent churches in providing material help
to the needy and seeking social justice? Or can some affluent churches
transcend the economic interests of their members and question the policies and practices that keep the rich rich and the poor poor? And if some
affluent churches are highly successful in one or both of these areas, what is
so special about them? How can we account for the success of some and the
ineffectiveness of others?

## Exploring the Issues

With encouragement from Robert Lynn and a grant from the Lilly
Endowment, we designed a study of affluent congregations[1] to explore the

above issues. Between 1984 and 1987 we studied thirty-one affluent churches in South Bend and Lafayette, Indiana (Davidson, Mock, and Johnson, 1988; Mock, Davidson, and Johnson, 1988; Johnson, Mock, and Davidson, 1988). Of these thirty-one churches, four were Roman Catholic; three were Episcopal; four were Presbyterian; six, United Methodist; five, Lutheran (including two Missouri Synod congregations); two, Christian (Disciples of Christ); two, Baptist (one American and one Southern); two, Church of the Brethren; and three, United Church of Christ.

We gathered an unusually rich combination of qualitative and quantitative data in these churches. We conducted extensive interviews with all the senior pastors and several associate pastors, as well as having them fill out a questionnaire. We collected parish budgets, mission statements, lists of programs, and occasional newsletters and bulletins. Finally, we asked individual members to complete a lengthy questionnaire.[2] These data provided us with an excellent opportunity to explore the questions raised above. This chapter summarizes our findings concerning the involvement of affluent churches in nurturing faith and promoting greater social justice. We begin by examining their involvement in nurturing faith.

## Nurturing Faith

Two major findings are most striking concerning affluent churches' involvement in faith. First, in direct opposition to common assumptions, the churches on the whole were highly involved in nurturing faith. Rather than lacking spiritual vitality, as we expected, many of the churches seemed to cultivate it to a significant degree; a few were marked by an abundance of vitality. Second, we were impressed with the wide range of faith involvement across these churches. Some were highly involved and effective in nurturing faith; and, at the other extreme, some had invested few of their abundant resources in the task and had been relatively unsuccessful in their efforts. The central tendencies and variations among these churches deserve closer examination.

Overall, these affluent churches invested a considerable portion of their resources in the nurturing of faith. On the average, they sponsored seven distinct programs oriented to nurturing faith and allocated 5 percent of their annual program budgets to these activities (not including staff salaries). Furthermore, the clergy of these affluent churches devoted an average of 54 percent of their professional staff time to nurturing the faith of their parishioners.

Faith was an integral part of the lives of these affluent church members. In the typical church, well over 80 percent of the members agreed with the statement, "Religion is an important part of my life." Sixty-five percent agreed with the statement, "I carry my faith over into all my other dealings in life." The members of these churches were also highly involved in religious activities. For instance, an average of 70 percent reported attending worship on a weekly basis, while approximately 80 percent reported praying privately outside of worship during the week.

The members of these churches also stated—with some regularity—that their church had been highly influential in the maturation of their personal faith. Overall, two-thirds of the members of these churches reported that worship and their pastor had had a "positive influence" on their personal faith. On the average, nearly half the members noted that their churches' Christian education programs, retreats, revivals, workshops, and fellowship activities had had a similar influence on their faith development.

These affluent churches thus were significantly more faith-oriented and their members more committed to and involved in faith than commonly thought. Many of these churches had invested significant proportions of their programmatic, staff, and financial resources to the nurturing of faith; their members often attended worship and prayed privately outside of worship; and members reported that their church had had a profound positive influence on their faith. Yet significant differences—far greater than the prevailing image—also separated the churches.

For example, the churches were not all equally invested in faith programs and activities. Some churches had developed as many as ten programs and invested as much as 10 percent of their budgets and 75 percent of their staff time to the strengthening of members' faith. Other churches devoted less than 1 percent of their budgets, a third of their staff time, and very few programs to enhancing spiritual vitality.

Nor were the members of these churches equally involved in religion. In churches where members were most highly involved, over 90 percent of the members agreed that religion was an important part of their lives, over 80 percent said their faith carried over into other aspects of their lives, more than 80 percent attended weekly worship, and over 90 percent prayed privately outside of worship. In the least involved churches, only a quarter of the members said that religion was important to them, less than 10 percent said that it affected other parts of their lives, only about half attended worship weekly, and about two-thirds prayed frequently outside of worship.

There was variation also in the churches' influence on the faith of their members. In general, members of the "most effective" churches were two to three times as likely as members of the "least effective" churches to report that their pastor, worship/Mass, and Christian education had played very positive roles in the maturation of their faith. For example, while nearly two-thirds in some churches said that their pastor had contributed to their faith, in other churches less than a third noted such a contribution.

Although these affluent churches were more heavily involved in nurturing faith than anticipated, our most striking finding was the considerable differences in levels of faith involvement across the thirty-one churches. The churches exhibited a wide range in the level of their congregational investments in faith, the religious salience and participation of their members, and the reported effectiveness of the church in nurturing faith. Some churches—in accordance with the prevailing image of affluent churches— invested few resources in faith and were seen as relatively ineffective by members, and those members found little importance in religion and its rituals. Other churches—almost in direct defiance of conventional wisdom—maintained intense faith programs backed by sizable resources. They contributed significantly and positively to the faith development of members, and their members were intensely involved in religion.

*Explaining the Differences*

Why were some affluent churches and their members much more heavily involved in faith than others? What is it that encourages success for some of the churches and not for others? Our analyses led us to discover four major factors that influence congregational involvement in faith: the location of the church, the occupational classes of members, the ideological ethos of members, and the ratio of giving to income within the congregation.

*Location.* As mentioned earlier, we studied affluent congregations in two Indiana cities: Lafayette and South Bend. These two cities were chosen for the marked social and cultural differences between them. Lafayette is a largely white, Anglo-Saxon, Protestant community that emphasizes the legitimacy of traditional institutions and values—including the church and religious values. Residents of Lafayette tend to stress the importance of being American, voting Republican, and disliking unions and welfare. South Bend is much more racially, ethnically, and religiously diverse and less bound by mainstream traditionalism. Citizens of South Bend tend to be more pro-union, pro-welfare, and pro-Democratic than their Lafayette neighbors.

Apparently the social homogeneity and cultural traditionalism of Lafayette are more conducive to the nurturing of faith than the heterogeneity and cultural marginalism of South Bend. Of the fifteen Lafayette churches, six scored high on our measures of faith involvement and only one scored low. In South Bend, nine of sixteen churches scored low, and only four scored high. Possibly, as Berger (1967:127) and others have noted, religious and cultural pluralism may lead to a "secularization of consciousness"—religious traditions are no longer absolute in the face of a multitude of worldviews. Congregations are thus able to nurture faith more readily where such social and cultural pluralism is diminished.

*Congregational Ethos.* In a similar vein, congregations—like cities—can be differentiated in terms of the social characteristics and cultural worldviews of their members. For instance, social and religious beliefs of the members can differ significantly from congregation to congregation. The members of some congregations may stress more liberal beliefs, including the ideas that to be Christian one must work for social justice, and that poverty is the result of structural barriers to success. More conservative churches tend to stress more individualistic beliefs, such as the idea that personal success is a sign of God's blessing to the deserving, and that poverty derives from the laziness and inferior ability of the poor.

Interestingly, both liberal and conservative churches tend to promote faith, though liberal churches are a bit more involved than conservative ones. Five of eight liberal churches and five of twelve conservative churches were highly involved and effective in nurturing faith.

Pluralist churches, a third type of church we have identified, are marked by a wide diversity of religious and social beliefs among members. These churches had the greatest difficulty in the area of faith: seven of eleven pluralist churches scored low on our measures of faith, and none of them scored high. Much like the effect of cultural pluralism in South Bend, the diversity of social and religious belief found in pluralist churches was not conducive to the effective cultivation of faith. Whether liberal or conservative, consensus of religious and social belief within the church seemingly provides more fertile ground for the growth of faith.

*Occupation.* Congregations are also differentiated across various social characteristics, such as gender, education, and occupation. The occupational profiles of our thirty-one affluent churches seemed closely related to their faith involvements. People's locations in the occupational class structure of society influence many aspects of their daily lives, including their religious orientations and thus the priorities and investments of their churches. A high proportion of homemakers (and to a lesser extent students) in a church was strongly associated with high involvement in faith, while a high proportion of business owners, managers, and professionals seemed to strongly discourage such involvement.

People who are not actively in the work force of society tend to hold little status or power in society and lack much control over the major events of their lives. Such people often compensate for their lack of power and control through an emphasis on receiving the riches of heaven through salvation from the evil ways of this world. As Weber (1964:106) states, "What [disprivileged classes] cannot claim to be, they replace by the worth of that which they will one day become, to which they will be called in some future life here or hereafter." Marx would undoubtedly refer to such an emphasis on the compensation of salvation as a "false consciousness" that blinds the disprivileged to the harsh realities of their lives and thus quells their radical potential. Be that as it may, the propensity of low-power, low-status groups to emphasize the idea of salvation encourages those churches with relatively high proportions of such individuals to be highly involved in faith.

Business people tend to have a far different outlook on life and religion. Belonging to the business elite—owners, managers, and professionals in business—means being oriented toward the acquisition of capital, status, and power, and stressing the instrumental values of pride, self-sufficiency, and efficiency. Under these conditions, religion and religious faith often come to be seen as largely irrelevant. As Weber (1964:107) has noted, elites are highly unlikely to develop a concept of salvation but rather use religion more to "legitimize" their privileged standing.[3] Churches with a large proportion of business elites thus tend to have difficulty investing in and involving their members in the cultivation of faith.

*Giving.* Giving, as a proportion of members' incomes, was also associated with a church's involvement in faith. The members of highly involved churches reported giving 4 percent of their incomes to the church annually, while giving in other churches averaged just under 3 percent. One highly involved church had a 6 percent rate of giving. Whether generous giving is an outcome of effective faith ministry or a significant impetus to such a ministry is always open to debate. Yet without adequate financial resources, churches may find it difficult to sponsor solid faith programs and hire the necessary leadership to develop and implement them. Therefore, churches whose leaders are successful in mobilizing the economic resources of members are bound to be more effective in nurturing the faith of their members.

*Implications*

These findings have several implications for the church and church leaders. First, though there were exceptions, most of the affluent churches we studied were not the spiritual black holes they were thought to be. On the whole, they had invested substantial resources in several faith programs. They had exerted a positive influence on the faith of their members, and those members were actively involved in the activities of a faith that was salient to their lives.

Second, and even more significant, large differences in faith involvement were exhibited by the churches. In explaining these differences, we found that affluent churches highly involved in faith tended to be located in traditional, rather than pluralistic, cities; possessed a well-defined rather than a more ambiguous congregational ethos; had large numbers of homemakers and relatively few business elites; and had members who gave generously to the church.

Interestingly, a series of leadership factors—such as the quality of pastoral and lay leadership as reported by members, or the pastor's theology—had no significant association with a congregation's involvement in faith. Not leaders and leadership processes but the physical location of affluent churches, their internal ethos, and the types of people who attend them were the crucial influences that seemed to dictate levels of church involvement in faith.

In an age when the mainline churches have sought to celebrate social and cultural pluralism within their congregations and to integrate their pews, it is not easy to accept the discovery that tradition and consensus provide more fertile soil for spiritual growth—and thus maybe growth in numbers. Regional and local church leaders are not likely to seek greater uniformity within their parishes.

There are limits to what church leaders could do about these relatively fixed and stable conditions of church life, even if they wanted to. Pluralism in American cities is hardly on the decline. Substantially altering the beliefs and values of church members, if not impossible, requires high-energy leadership and vast resources. To push for conformity and to quell dissent in the church are not acceptable to most clergy and laity. Further, to focus new-member recruitment on particular occupational groups would cut deeply across the grain of universalism in the church; and few are ready to reject the business elites and their potentially large contributions.

Yet leaders' anxiety over these issues runs high, particularly in light of the decline of the mainline churches since the 1950s. And apparently little can be done to alleviate this anxiety. However, the substantial efforts and effectiveness of the majority of our thirty-one affluent churches in nurturing the faith of their members should help ease the worries of these leaders. If affluent churches of the mainline—those churches least expected by lay people, scholars, and prophets alike to inspire true spiritual vitality—can generate such vitality, their leaders should be heartened to learn that faith and spirituality are not limited to the more evangelical churches but also run strong within the mainline.

## Social Ministry

The story of social ministry in these affluent churches reads quite differently. Affluent churches, on the whole, simply are not as engaged in social ministry as in nurturing the faith of their members. In accordance with popular wisdom, most affluent churches do very little to alleviate the plight of the disadvantaged through charitable services or to promote the social change necessary for greater equality and justice.

Yet a few affluent churches are actively involved in providing social services and advocating the rights of the disadvantaged. As was the case for involvement in faith, levels of involvement in social ministry vary significantly across affluent churches. Much as Hadden and Longino (1974) and Smith (1981) found, a number of our affluent churches have turned concern for the poor, hungry, and unemployed into active involvement in seeking greater equality and justice.

Furthermore, the more fixed and stable characteristics of these churches—such as location, ethos, and members' social class—played little role in levels of involvement in social ministry. Rather, efforts in social ministry appeared more dependent on various aspects of leadership and leadership processes.

In general, the churches we studied did not invest their resources as heavily in serving the needy and advocating the rights of the disadvantaged as they did in nurturing the faith of members. For instance, only two of the churches had a paid staff member whose principal responsibilities were for social outreach programs. Yet most of the churches had at least two paid staff persons working in the area of faith (i.e., a senior pastor and an associate or Christian education director). Thus, on the average, clergy and other professional staff devoted 54 percent of their professional time to nurturing faith and less than 15 percent to social concerns.

Furthermore, the typical affluent church allocated significantly more of its program budget to worship and Christian education than to outreach, and it sponsored about twice as many faith-oriented programs as outreach programs within the church. However, these churches also contributed financial support to an average of four outreach programs organized by other organizations, such as local ecumenical urban ministries and the Salvation Army. Yet overall, these churches invested relatively little in social ministry.

Nor was social ministry a top priority for members of these affluent congregations. Although many members felt they were called as Christians to provide at least some assistance, relatively few gave a significant amount of their money, possessions, or time to helping the poor. For example, 24 percent of the members of these churches agreed that "helping the poor is central to my life," and 59 percent reported that they strive hard to provide help for the needy. Yet only 40 percent reported "often" donating money to help the poor, only 26 percent often donated material goods, and a mere 14 percent gave significant proportions of their time.

As with personal faith, these churches had heightened some members' interest in "building a more just world." On the average, 25 percent of the respondents noted that worship/Mass, their pastor, and their church's social ministry programs had been a "positive influence" on their interest in social ministry. This compares with over half who reported the strong positive influence of the church on their faith.

In many ways, then, the popular image of affluent churches as relatively unconcerned about the poor, hungry, unemployed, and oppressed appears to be fairly accurate. Most of these churches invested little of their programmatic, staff, and financial resources in active social outreach; their members, though somewhat concerned about the poor, had given little of themselves to helping the poor; and only a few members reported that their church had had a positive influence on their interest in seeking to promote greater justice and equality.

*Variations*

However, there was wide variation within this overall pattern. Some affluent churches were heavily involved in social ministry and some were less involved than the typical church. A few churches invested as much as

13 percent of their budgets and a third of their staff time to social ministry, conducted up to nine outreach programs on their own, and supported as many as thirteen other programs with the help of other organizations. Other churches were involved in only one or two outreach programs and invested less than one percent of their budgets and virtually no staff time to social ministry.

Involvement in social ministry also varied significantly across the membership of these churches. The members of some churches were quite enthusiastic about the prophetic role of the church. In these churches over half the members agreed that helping the poor was central to their lives, almost 60 percent often donated money, over 33 percent donated goods, and 25 percent donated time. In the least socially conscious churches, less than 20 percent felt that helping the poor was important and only 8 percent had often volunteered their time to such endeavors.

Nor were all the churches equally effective in strengthening their members' interest in building a more just world. As with church influence on personal faith, the members of "most effective" churches were two to three times as likely as the members of "least effective" churches to report that their pastor and worship/Mass had played an important role in heightening their interest in social ministry. Members of the most effective churches were five times as likely to note the positive influence of their churches' social ministry programs.

In sum, most affluent churches and their members appear to have only limited involvement in social ministry—far less involvement than they have in nurturing faith. Through an indifference to social problems, many of these churches seem quite willing to support the various policies and practices that maintain both the affluence of their members and the suffering of the poor. Yet to label all affluent churches as devoid of compassion is to deny the existence of the few affluent churches that are heavily involved in effective social activism. Although most affluent churches had low levels of involvement and a few had virtually none, several were highly involved—investing significant proportions of their resources in social ministry, having numerous members highly involved in social ministry, and effectively heightening an interest in promoting social justice.

### Explaining the Variations

Thus, as with these churches' faith life, we were confronted with the question, If most affluent churches were not highly involved in helping the poor, how were some able to become so involved?

Through our analyses we discovered six factors that have considerable impact on congregational involvement in social ministry, four of which are directly related to leadership and other congregational dynamics. Whereas faith seemed to arise quite naturally from a particular set of fixed and stable conditions (e. g., location in a more traditional city; a strong congregational ethos; few business elite), involvement in social ministry had much more to do with leadership in the congregation. If social ministry was to be an integral part of these congregations, strong, prophetic leadership was necessary to legitimize such activities to their affluent members. In other words, social ministry did not just happen; it took some doing. Certain congregational dynamics appear most critical for promoting social ministry in affluent churches.

*Pastor's Religious Orientation.* Through interviews and surveys, we were able to classify the theological orientations of the clergy of these churches and the frequency with which their sermons and teachings explicitly stated an interdependence between faith and social ministry. Pastors with more conservative theological orientations stressed the importance of personal faith, the saving of souls, and the comforting nature of religion, and seldom related the teachings of faith to social concerns. From this orientation, concern for the poor and disadvantaged develops within the faithful individual; by changing people, we change society.

The more moderate theological orientation of some clergy emphasized the idea that faith is a gift, not something to be earned through "good works." While a strong personal faith is still the key to the Christian life within the moderate orientation, there is a greater recognition of believers' obligation to care about the poor and powerless than within the conservative theology. The sermons of moderate pastors several times a year directly linked together the call to be faithful and the call to be helpful to those in need.

Liberal pastors were more inclined to stress the inseparability of faith and social ministry. The church and its members live the faith through working for social justice. These pastors tend to emphasize the prophetic and challenging aspects of Christianity as much as its comforting nature. Their sermons frequently discussed how living the faith means serving others. Some liberal pastors often said that involvement in social ministry can greatly deepen faith.

While neither the ideological ethos of members nor their occupations influence their churches' involvement in social ministry (as was the case for faith), the religious orientations of their pastors did. Congregations with liberal pastors were far more involved in social ministry than congregations with conservative pastors. Of fourteen congregations with liberal pastors, eight scored high on involvement in social ministry; three of the four congregations with conservative pastors scored low on involvement in outreach and none scored high. Two of thirteen churches with moderate pastors scored high and six scored low. By drawing a strong theological link between faith and social action in their sermons, religious education classes, and newsletters, liberal pastors appear more willing and able to encourage their congregations to become involved in social ministry. When the interdependence of faith and action is not articulated, involvement in social ministry tends to wane significantly or never develop.

*Quality of Lay and Pastoral Leadership.* Strong lay and pastoral leadership is also crucial to encouraging church involvement in social ministry. When members perceive their leaders as having many talents and abilities to lead, as taking their leadership responsibility seriously, as having made several good decisions, and as having good rapport with members and each other, the involvement of the church and its members in social ministry tends to be high. Eight of sixteen churches reporting strong leadership were highly involved in social ministry and only three scored low. Of fifteen churches where members lacked confidence in their leaders, seven scored low in involvement in outreach and only two were highly involved.

Leadership, then, appears to be critical to church involvement in service and justice issues. For the affluent church to invest its resources in outreach programs against the economic interests of members requires not only clergy with a strong prophetic message but quality clergy and lay leaders who are perceived as trustworthy, responsible, and able to lead the church in new and exciting directions.

*Sense of Community.* One other dynamic of affluent congregations played an important role in their involvement in social outreach: the sense of community within the congregation. In churches where members cared for and felt a special bond with one another, involvement of the church and members in social ministry was high. Where a sense of intimacy and familylike feelings were lacking, so was concern for the needy outside the church. Half the churches with a strong sense of community were highly involved in social ministry. Only two of fifteen churches lacking strong community had similar levels of involvement and seven appeared virtually uninterested in social concerns. Caring within the walls of the church seems to significantly spill over into caring for the disadvantaged in the world.

*Denominational Theology and Education.* Although the congregational dynamics of leadership and community appeared to have the most influence, two more fixed aspects of these churches also affected their level of involvement in assisting the needy and seeking justice: denominational theology and the proportion of members educated in business.

We categorized denominational theology much as we did pastors' religious orientation: conservative, moderate, and liberal.[4] Congregations in theologically liberal denominations tended to be far more involved than churches from more conservative denominational traditions. Eight of nineteen churches in liberal denominations were highly involved in social action. All three of the churches from conservative denominations scored low on our measures of involvement.

We also categorized the educational backgrounds of church members into one of four types: business, the natural sciences and technology, the social sciences, and the humanities. Having a high proportion of members educated in business and management tended to thwart social ministry, though having a large proportion of business leaders in the church did not.

### Implications

Several key conclusions can be drawn from our discoveries about the involvement of affluent churches in faith and social ministry. First, affluent churches and their members are much more oriented toward nurturing faith than toward promoting justice in their communities, their nation, or their world.[5] Although fairly heavily invested in nurturing the faith of members, affluent churches typically invest little capital and little time to helping the poor and reforming injustice. Their members, though cognitively concerned about the poor and hungry, tend to contribute little money or material goods, and particularly little time to social ministry programs. When these churches have designed programs of social outreach, most of these programs tend to offer simple services to the needy that provide only short-term alleviation of problems. Seldom do their programs confront root causes of social problems and seek long-term solutions.

Much as common wisdom holds, the affluence and political control wielded by the members of these churches tend to limit beliefs and priorities conducive to strong efforts to feed the hungry, clothe the naked, and advocate the rights of disadvantaged groups. Although most affluent churches maintain a few programs of assistance, programs that seek to reduce injustice by questioning the legitimacy of policies that help maintain the affluence and power of these members in their communities are few and far between. Such programs confront too directly the economic and political interests of many of the members of affluent congregations.

A second finding, however, may be even more important: a small number of affluent churches are not only heavily involved in service activities, but have also begun to fight the many injustices that keep the poor poor. These affluent churches seem to have overcome the economic and political interests of their members and have begun to rock the boat when their affluent neighbors will not. The crucial factor in their involvement seems to be strong, prophetic leadership. When pastors clearly articulate that "you shall love the Lord with all your heart and soul and mind, and your neighbor as yourself" (see Matt. 22:37–39), and when pastors and lay leaders are perceived as effective, responsible, and even visionary, affluent churches and their members become significantly more involved in the social problems of our times.

Leaders of affluent churches are faced with an inherent conflict between the privileged status of their members and the prophetic role of the church. The church's involvement in challenging the legitimacy of policies that maintain large disparities of wealth in society may run directly counter to the economic and political interests of many members. Clergy and lay leaders thus have a choice. They can reflect and reinforce their members' reluctance to do social ministry, or they can challenge the congregation to become involved.

Even against the lure of money and the seduction of power, a union of clergy and lay leaders with a strong prophetic message can lead their affluent churches and members "to do justice, and to love kindness, and to walk humbly with [their] God" (Micah 6:8).

## NOTES

1. We included only congregations that had a higher than average proportion of affluent members. In 1985, when the bulk of our data was gathered, 59 percent of the members of the thirty-one churches had gone to college, compared with 36 percent of the U.S. population as a whole. Forty-nine percent either owned or managed businesses or were professionals, compared with 24 percent of all Americans. Fifty-two percent had family incomes of $30,000 or more, compared with 45 percent of the country as a whole. Twenty-four percent had incomes in excess of $50,000, compared with 18 percent of all Americans.

2. The members' questionnaire yielded a 51 percent response rate.

3. Karl Marx would also term the elites' use of religion to legitimize their privileged position and power as "false consciousness," since—at least to Marx—

no adequate legitimacy exists for anyone to possess such privilege and power when others do not.

4. The Lutheran Church–Missouri Synod and the Southern Baptist Convention were categorized as theologically conservative; the United Methodist Church, the Evangelical Lutheran Church in America, the American Baptist Churches, and the Christian Church (Disciples of Christ) were considered moderate; and the Church of the Brethren, the Roman Catholic Church, the Presbyterian Church (U.S.A.), and the United Church of Christ were considered liberal.

5. There was virtually no association between our two overall measures of faith and social ministry ($r = -.05$). For instance, only three of our thirty-one churches scored high on both involvement in faith and in social ministry. By and large, what affluent churches achieved in one area was no indication of how well they succeeded in the other.

## WORKS CITED

Berger, Peter
    1967        *The Sacred Canopy*. New York: Doubleday.

Birch, Bruce C., and Larry L. Rasmussen
    1978        *The Predicament of the Prosperous*. Philadelphia: Westminster Press.

Davidson, James D.
    1985        *Mobilizing Social Movement Organizations*. West Lafayette, Ind.: Society for the Scientific Study of Religion.

Davidson, James D., Alan K. Mock, and C. Lincoln Johnson
    1988        "Affluent Churches: Nurturing Faith and Promoting Justice." A final report to Lilly Endowment, Inc.

Driggers, B. Carlisle
    1979        *Models of Metropolitan Ministry*. Nashville: Broadman Press.

Hadden, Jeffrey K., and Charles Longino
    1974        *Gideon's Gang*. Philadelphia: Pilgrim Press.

Johnson, C. Lincoln, James D. Davidson, and Alan K. Mock
    forthcoming  *Faith and Social Ministry: Ten Perspectives*. Chicago: Loyola University Press.

Mock, Alan K., James D. Davidson, and C. Lincoln Johnson
    1988        "Social Differentiation and Individual Belief: Affluent Christians' Beliefs About Inequality." A final report to Lilly Endowment, Inc.

Pope, Liston
    1942        *Millhands and Preachers*. New Haven, Conn.: Yale University Press.

Roozen, David A., William McKinney, and Jackson W. Carroll
    1984        *Varieties of Religious Presence*. New York: Pilgrim Press.

Smith, Donald
    1981          *Congregations Alive*. Philadelphia: Westminster Press.

Sweetser, Thomas
    1983          *Successful Parishes*. Minneapolis: Winston Press.

Weber, Max
    1964          *The Sociology of Religion*. Trans. Ephraim Fischoff. New York:
                  Free Press of Glencoe.

Winter, Gibson
    1962          *The Suburban Captivity of the Churches*. New York: Macmil-
                  lan Co.

# SIX

# Congregational Self-Images for Social Ministry
## CARL S. DUDLEY AND SALLY A. JOHNSON

Congregational self-images are both the mirror in which the members see themselves and, in turn, the shape they give to the church. A congregation that sees itself as a "big church" may have confidence in its own resources that can sustain a variety of ministries; yet that sense of bigness may allow members to feel anonymous and hide in the crowd rather than become actively involved. The "small church," on the other hand, which may enjoy its intimacy, may let the feeling of "smallness" limit its programming. A "neighborhood church" feels that it knows the people and problems of its turf, while a "tall-steeple church" may be proud of its grand Gothic arches and large pipe organ. These images reflect some of the values and commitments of church members.

Names that draw on scriptural images carry their own kind of power. Church names like Calvary, Bethel, or Zion were chosen to evoke biblical stories. The ministry project named The Mustard Seed expects to grow quietly yet irresistibly. Strong and compelling congregational self-images bind members together, expressing their shared identity and delineating the ways they differ from others.

The most powerful bonds often remain unspoken. Most compelling—for good or for ill—are the silent assumptions based in shared values, experiences, habits, and relationships. When a congregation discovers symbols that articulate its identity, it can build on its strengths and address its weaknesses. The best self-images affirm the values that bind the members, give sharpness and meaning to areas of disagreement, and provide a context for change and growth.

Theologians and sociologists have clustered church images in typologies to describe patterns of belief and ministry by which congregations serve the Lord. These typologies have been based on such factors as size, social context, and organizational dynamics.[1] Other, more popularly recognized images have been suggested by church leaders and reinforced by the mass media. The self-image of an evangelical church encourages its members to talk about their faith with others, while members of a liberal church expect to be tolerant of wide differences among themselves and in their communities.

In the past three years we have had access to a wide spectrum of congregations, learning from them the images in which they see themselves and how those images are related to the roles they play in their communities. With a grant from the Lilly Endowment and with the encouragement of Robert W. Lynn, senior vice-president for religion, we have been able to seed forty congregation-based social ministry projects in the Midwest. These projects are sponsored by Roman Catholic and Protestant churches from more than a dozen denominations, roughly typical of mainline and some evangelical congregations in Chicago, central Illinois, Indianapolis, and northern Indiana.

Drawing on narratives written by the people themselves, we have identified five types of congregational self-images. We have supplemented their stories with written survey questions, interviews with church leaders, and observations of their development of social ministry projects. These are not the only images that could be identified, but they reflect five different and effective ways these congregations relate to their communities as they remember their stories. First we will introduce and summarize these types as previously reported,[2] and then we will explain with more recent data the ways they shape their social ministries.

## Five Congregational Self-Images

*The survivor church* tells of the crises it has weathered. Most often these have been struggles internal to the church, though some congregations share this identity by virtue of being a gathering of people who have survived other perils. Survivor churches are reactive, and always on the verge of being overwhelmed by emergencies. They do not expect to conquer their problems, but they will not give in. They are determined rather than domineering, relentless rather than aggressive. They hang on long after others would have quit, because "we've made it through worse than this before." Although outsiders have often seen these churches as "weak," we find this self-image to be remarkably resilient and productive when leaders learn to make positive use of their crises.

*The crusader church* never tires of seeking out issues and championing causes. Crusader churches are the high-profile congregations against which the social commitment of other churches is sometimes measured. Independent, often entrepreneurial in style, they are largely made up of members who have chosen the church for the stands it takes and the causes it pursues. Crusaders share with survivors a high level of commitment and energy, although the crusader differs by being proactive in its approach to problems. We have found these highly visible congregations to be significantly different from their familiar stereotypes.

*The pillar church* is anchored in its community and feels a distinct responsibility for it. The architecture often reflects this self-image—strong pillars that lift the roof physically and the community spiritually. The building may be modest in a small town, or imposing in a neighborhood that expects a prominent architectural posture. Like the building, the members are pillars of the community, good citizens individually and corporately. More than the building, they share a pillar mind-set. Resources of heritage, experience, or money are to be used for the good of all.

*The pilgrim church* tells of the movements of cultural groups in its history, in counterpoint to the pillar's sense of being rooted in a place. Most pilgrim congregations have seen waves of immigration or racial change, and often "old ethnics" and "new ethnics" now share the story. These are the Slovaks or Swedes whose neighborhood now receives Mexicans or Asians, the interracial parish with Italian and German roots, the black adherents of a largely white evangelical tradition. Another kind of pilgrim congregation recites its own life story move by move, from one dwelling place to another. For pilgrim congregations, their culture and their Christian faith are woven into a single fabric.

*The servant church*, finally, goes about the work of helping people in need with a quiet faithfulness. They are neither threatened like survivors nor aggressive like crusaders. Where pillars feel responsible for the whole community and pilgrims respond to distinct groups, servants see individuals in need and reach out to help them in supportive and pastoral ways. Servant churches are sustained by servant people—those who visit the sick, take meals to the bereaved, and send cards to shut-ins. From there it is a natural extension for them to provide food, clothing, and other basic needs to their neighbors. Their faith is lived out in service.

In summary, the images may be understood by their primary style of response to human need:

Survivor: Is reactive to the crises of an overwhelming world
Crusader: Is proactive to translate crises into causes

Pillar: Takes civic responsibility that embraces the community
Pilgrim: Cares for extended family or cultural group
Servant: Provides support for individuals who need help

Some congregations fit easily within one self-image, but most churches have elements of several. The pastor or lay leaders may hold a different image than the members at large. Age groups or other segments of the congregation may see the church through different lenses. The dominant self-image of the congregation may have changed over the years with shifts in circumstances and membership.

One church in our study is seen as a survivor by denominational staff who have debated closing it for years; yet the members see themselves as pilgrims historically who are now crusaders in their neighborhood. Another church is proud to be an innovative crusader in its community, yet a pillar style of worship provides an important source of unity and energy. A congregation with impressive architecture and a downtown location looks like a pillar, feels like a group of pilgrims with survivor undertones, and has energetic crusader leaders.

From our experience, tensions between these images can be creative, and need not be destructive. Leaders who recognize the variety of self-images can help to set diversity in positive perspective. Differences among individuals and between congregations can be constructively channeled— when and if they are understood. Church officers, pastors, and consultants who appreciate these differences can give leadership that is uniquely appropriate to each congregation. With an understanding of biblical and theological foundations for each, all five approaches can invigorate healthy congregations, and all five can motivate and give focus to social ministry. But they do it differently, each with its own style.

## Images for Social Ministry

These five self-images all assume different ways of relating to the community. We have explored possible implications for a church's mission orientation and response, its leadership style, the ways it goes about forming community partnerships, its theological and social beliefs, its decision-making and sense of group cohesion, and its readiness to venture into social justice advocacy along with service. While some of our findings have supported traditional assumptions, others have surprised us—and may liberate church leaders from some negative stereotypes regarding social ministries (see Table 6.1).

## TABLE 6.1

## Churches by Self-Image

| CHARACTERISTICS OF CONGREGATIONS | SURVIVOR | CRUSADER | PILLAR | PILGRIM | SERVANT | N* |
|---|---|---|---|---|---|---|
| PARTNERS: Average (mean) number of partners per church. (Churches, Nonchurch partners, Total) | C .44<br>N .22<br>T .67 | C 1.33<br>N 2.67<br>T 4.00 | C 2.00<br>N .73<br>T 2.73 | C .67<br>N .50<br>T 1.17 | C 1.50<br>N .13<br>T 1.63 | (40) |
| CONGREGATIONAL THEOLOGY: Views on biblical authority and salvation. (Evangelical, Moderate, Liberal) | E 44%<br>M 44%<br>L 11% | E 33%<br>M 33%<br>L 33% | E 0%<br>M 36%<br>L 64% | E 17%<br>M 67%<br>L 17% | E 0%<br>M 63%<br>L 38% | (40) |

| MEMBERS' PERCEPTIONS OF THEIR CONGREGATIONS | SURVIVOR<br>1 | CRUSADER<br>2 | PILLAR<br>3 | PILGRIM<br>4 | SERVANT<br>5 | N | PAIRS SIGNIF. AT P < .01** |
|---|---|---|---|---|---|---|---|
| INTIMACY: Scale measuring social cohesion of congregation. Higher score = greater sense of intimacy. | 11.5 | 11.8 | 11.5 | 11.7 | 10.2 | (3939) | 5 < 1,2,3,4 |
| DECISION-MAKING: Scale measuring views of congregational decision-making process. Higher score = more open, participatory process. | 16.1 | 15.7 | 14.9 | 15.1 | 14.6 | (3076) | 1 > 3,4,5<br>2 > 3,5 |

| | 1 | 2 | 3 | 4 | 5 | (N) | |
|---|---|---|---|---|---|---|---|
| ACTIVISM: Individual conscience vs. corporate congregational action on social issues. Scale from $1.0$ = individual to $7.0$ = corporate. | 3.9 | 4.4 | 3.5 | 3.7 | 3.6 | (3783) | $2 > 1,3,4,5$<br>$1 > 3,5$ |
| ADVOCACY: Scale measuring priority given to church's advocacy for social justice issues. Higher score = greater priority. | 10.7 | 11.0 | 10.3 | 11.0 | 10.6 | (3771) | $3 < 1,2,4$<br>$5 < 2,4$ |
| PARTICIPATION: Scale measuring members' participation in social ministry. Higher score = greater participation. | 4.8 | 5.4 | 4.6 | 5.5 | 4.0 | (2999) | $5 < 1,2,3,4$<br>$1,3 < 2,4$ |
| SOCIAL ATTITUDES: Scale measuring members' orientation to social issues. Higher score = more liberal. | 13.0 | 13.5 | 12.0 | 14.1 | 12.1 | (3818) | $3 < 1,2,4$<br>$5 < 1,2,4$<br>$1 < 4$ |
| GOD OF JUSTICE: Percent agreeing that the church should work for justice. | 32% | 32% | 22% | 33% | 21% | (3953) | *** |

* The first two items consider the forty churches as the units of analysis, while the remainder are based on individual-level church member data. In the latter, respondents' scores are weighted according to size of church sample, so that each church receives equal weight in the analysis.

** The test used to determine significance for these items is a one-way analysis of variance. Scheffe multiple comparison test used for testing any two pairs of means.

*** Tested using chi-square test; significant at $< 0.01$ level.

These five congregational types appear to cut across denominational and theological spectra. Of the forty churches we have studied, eight to eleven fall in each group (including five churches that share equally in two identities and are profiled in both). There are at least six different denominations represented in each type, including Roman Catholics and Protestants in all types. Evangelicals, moderates, and liberals were well represented throughout the types. Most congregations showed elements of more than one self-image, usually with one predominating. The forty churches in our study provided living stories from which we draw these five self-images.

## Survivor Churches: Against All Odds

Survivor congregations feel overwhelmed in a world beyond their control. Driven by the needs they have experienced and the troubles they have endured, they feel they are moving from one crisis to the next, one step ahead of disaster. Equally influenced by tradition and by contemporary trends, they are pulled by both forces and stabilized by neither. Pastors and active lay leaders often feel both psychologically and spiritually overworked and undernourished. Fatigue and burnout haunt these ministries.

When survivors look toward their communities, it is with the same sense of being overwhelmed that they have experienced in their own internal struggles. Often they are located in declining or impoverished neighborhoods (not unrelated to their own decline), and the social problems seem too great and complicated to conquer. Rather than withdraw, however, the survivor starts someplace and tries to make a dent in the situation.

These churches can do more than just survive. They can become sources of individual help and catalysts for social change. The survivors in our group have come to view their hardships and struggles not just as liabilities but as grist for the mill of ministry. Crisis gives them an identity. In reacting to their conditions, they have learned to use the pressure of negative circumstances as a positive motivating force to generate ministry.

They may be reacting with their backs to the wall, but it works. These are activist congregations, second only to the crusaders in their corporate commitment to respond to social problems. They are also close-knit groups with a strong sense of their own communal bonds and highly participative decision-making. Most of our survivors are evangelicals and moderates.

Though it would seem that they need all the help they can get, the survivor congregations in our group have formed the fewest community partnerships for ministry. When they do, they turn to safe and familiar partners, such as churches on the same corner or of the same denomination. It may be a sense of isolation and precarious existence that makes them unwilling or unable to risk new alliances. It may also be part of their long-conditioned pattern of resolutely slogging through the swamp. They have made it through worse before, and they "keep on keeping on."

Sometimes well-meaning advisors are tempted to urge pastors and lay leaders of survivor churches to set more realistic goals. But in our experience, many of these leaders seem built for crisis ministries. They have the gift of long-suffering commitment, and often the gift of arousing others as well. They can use crises to generate energy, recruit volunteers, and raise money. Crises provide people for their prayers and a pitch for their sermons. Often tired, always overextended, these congregations find their identity in survival—and they will not give up.

## Crusader Churches: Tackling the World

The dominant public image of a church in social ministry has often been the crusader congregation. Assertive, restless, ready to risk all for a cause, these churches have been the battering ram of social justice issues. More influenced by new trends than by tradition, these groups are the most independent of other authority, including denominational ties. They need and produce strong, dramatic leaders with sharp ideas, and those leaders hold their primary loyalty.

Crusaders are proactive, where survivors are reactive. As the survivor church is driven by crises within, the crusader is activated by crises without—and sees in every crisis a larger cause. Run-down homes signal community decline, and their repair represents more than bricks and paint. A victimized woman brings vivid consciousness of widespread spousal abuse, and sheltering her family is a step toward sheltering all. Of the five types, crusaders have the greatest activist identity, taking corporate stands on justice issues, and they have the strongest conviction that those stands are required by their faith in a God of justice.

Members of crusader congregations participate more actively in social ministries than do members of most other types of churches. Their sense of inner community is strong, and they are satisfied with their own decision-making systems. Crusader churches sustain a high energy level that mobilizes their own people and others around them. Aggressive and decisive, they often develop innovative responses to urgent community needs.

These churches are particularly resourceful in the coalitions they build.

Among the churches in our project, the crusaders have formed the most partnerships. In doing so, they are the least likely to stay within familiar networks and the most likely to develop functional and creative coalitions with service agencies, schools, hospitals, businesses, banks, and community organizations. Partners are allies in the fight for the cause at hand, and temporary coalitions are often built for specific purposes.

Contrary to some popular misconceptions, these socially active churches are not more likely to be theologically liberal. Only a few of the churches in our sample fall in the liberal category, while the majority are moderates and evangelicals. It may be that few liberal churches define issues clearly enough or risk faith so sharply as to become crusaders. It may also be that the crusader identity arises out of a level of energy and commitment that operates independently of traditional theological postures. However, although most crusaders are not theologically liberal, they do hold liberal views on social and political questions.

Crusader congregations have the strongest commitment to justice in their social ministries. They are among the most likely to see that social evils are caused by destructive systems as well as personal deficiencies, and their ministries of service move naturally into advocacy roles.

Although crusaders are proactive and survivors are reactive, they share a number of similarities. Both demand high levels of commitment, and both respond to community needs with a sense of urgency. Crisis motivates both: survivors cope with it and crusaders tackle it head on. The programs and processes they produce are very different, but the energy and commitment are surprisingly similar.

Crusaders typically form the front line of the church's social action—sensing the impending crises, generating interest in the issues, and shaping the theological and social science foundations for subsequent denominational involvement. Admirers are tempted to make them the normative model for congregational social ministry. Yet the majority of American Christian congregations build on other identities to generate effective social ministries.

## Pillar Churches: Solid as a Rock

Some churches clearly approach social ministry with a sense of Christian civic responsibility. Anchored in a place, with resources and status, they feel an obligation to work for the welfare of the community. Often pillar churches are named for their places or have "community" in their names.

They are the Methodist (or Baptist or Catholic—or Christian) presence on that side of town.

Most pillars are large or medium-sized congregations; they tend to have a relatively low sense of group intimacy and more limited participation in their decision-making. Pillar churches expect professional-quality leadership from both clergy and lay leaders. In seeking partners for ministry, they often turn to existing civic networks to which those leaders have connections. Pillars are second only to crusaders in the number of partners they recruit; but where crusaders have the most nonchurch partners, pillars draw the most churches. They often seem to approach partnering from a characteristic sense of strength, extending an opportunity to others to join with them in their community ministry.

Two-thirds of the pillars among our churches are theologically liberal, and one-third are moderate. Yet these churches' views on social issues are the most conservative. Contrary to what might be expected of these rooted, established congregations, they are the least tied to tradition and the most influenced by contemporary trends. Pillar churches are less convinced than others that their faith requires them to take corporate stands on justice issues, and are less inclined to do so. They tend to study an issue longer than other churches, and often they seem slow in making decisions—possibly because they recognize a variety of viewpoints and program options. But when mobilized, these churches can have a powerful impact.

In comparison with the crisis orientation of crusaders and survivors, pillar churches maintain their composure. Built on a rock, they feel no imminent threat to their own existence and offer a presence of stability to their neighborhood. They also offer shelter to a variety of community groups that use their facilities for meetings and activities. When invited to develop new social ministries, they survey their area broadly and identify widespread problems. They are the most apt to develop comprehensive responses to community needs. When a pillar chooses a target population—such as the deaf and hearing impaired, youth, or the elderly—it often tries to meet many of their needs all at once through a multifaceted program.

Though members of pillar churches have the least orientation to the systemic causes of social problems, these congregations are among the quickest to move into advocacy roles as they implement social ministry projects. Thorough and ambitious in their planning, they see themselves as community institutions, networking with other such institutions for the common good. Pillars have a quiet but firm commitment to duty. They live for the commendation in Matthew 25: "Well done, good and faithful servant."

## Pilgrim Churches: A People on a Journey

While pillar churches are built on a place, pilgrims are rooted in a people—often a people passing through a place. For most pilgrim churches, a cultural history colors their sense of identity. Many have seen several waves of immigration in their neighborhood and have faithfully adopted each group in their ministry. Little has been written about the social ministries of congregations with ethnic, national, and racial roots. As might be expected, the pilgrims in our study have a deep commitment to history and tradition, and have the strongest bonding as a church "family." Pilgrim churches seek "traditional" leaders, as tradition is defined and valued in each cultural group. These leaders are no less professionally qualified than those in pillar churches, but they are expected to function more as parent figures within the church family system—and, as such, must bear and honor the heritage.

Pilgrim churches carry a strong, moderate faith, and only a few liberal or evangelical groups are included in this type. Secure in their Christian-cultural roots, they are free to explore their differences. A black church is drawn to a largely white evangelical denomination by common bonds of a biblical foundation and personal theological freedom. A Slovakian-Mexican church tells of the excitement of worship when "the traditional organ music gives way to improvised mariachi of guitars and other contemporary instruments."

The pilgrim churches in our project have been nearly as slow as survivors in forming partnerships for ministry. When they do, they find partners in their extended family—groups that represent historic ties, neighborhood connections, or cultural networks. In partnerships as well as in leadership, the trusted relationship of *who* people are is more important than the functional relationship of *what* they do.

The pilgrim congregation's call to mission is different from the crisis orientation of the survivor and crusader. It shares with the pillar a sense of responsibility, but not for the community per se. Drawn mostly from populations that have been marginalized and oppressed in our culture, they have carried the responsibility for "our people." This is the black congregation helping black children to stay in school and achieve, or the Hispanic group teaching citizenship classes to more recent Hispanic immigrants.

There are also pilgrims in a second stage: the most urgent needs of their own group satisfied, they now extend their ministry to another group. The descendants of Scandinavian immigrants foster a new congregation of ethnic Chinese refugees from Indochina, and the two groups tell their common story in terms of the Exodus. In a neighborhood once called Stockholm, now a weekly drop-off point for new Mexican immigrants, "old ethnic" Anglos work with "new ethnic" Hispanics to offer educational opportunities to their Spanish-speaking neighbors.

Born of years of hard work to carve out a viable place in American society, the social ministries of pilgrim churches are oriented toward long-term improvement in people's lives and opportunities. Almost uniformly the pilgrims in our project have developed educational ministries—nurturing children, preparing youth, and training adults for jobs, as well as offering classes in the English language, citizenship, parenting, and other life skills. Their common motivation is to help "our people" make a better place in the land of opportunity—whether the people are "ours" by blood or by adoption.

At their best, pilgrims have a special gift: they are not limited by their own ethnic heritage, but broadened by it. Far from being cloistered, ghetto churches filling only their own needs, pilgrims use their own experiences to help them reach out to others. Though not inclined to think of themselves as "activists," they are among the most active in social ministries. Strong in the values they place on both local and global concerns, they hold the most liberal social attitudes. With the highest comprehension of the systemic dimensions of social problems, they are able to move into advocacy roles along with individual service. When their history is mobilized in ministry, they can become a powerful force for community-building.

## Servant Churches: Faithful Helpers

If high energy marks crusaders and survivors, and if pillars and pilgrims carry a sense of responsibility, then, by contrast, servant churches are characterized by moderation. These congregations are not inclined to carry anything to excess—in social causes, community programs, doctrinal commitments, or congregational intimacy. They are not moved to initiate crusades or campaigns but simply want to help people, and their social ministries have a distinct focus on the needs of individuals.

Of the five groups, servant churches are the most influenced by history and tradition. For them, caring for people seems the most basic and natural consequence of their Christian faith. This sense of servanthood may be the most widespread and universal foundation for generating social ministries.

Just as their ministries are focused on particular persons in need, these congregations are themselves gatherings of individuals. Statistically they have uniquely low feelings of group cohesiveness and report that their decision-making process is limited to relatively few members. Yet their leaders tend to be caring, supportive, and pastoral, with a conscious focus on enabling individuals to reach their potential. Servant congregations are composed of gathered individuals who know they need each other, who reach out to help others like themselves—people, not systems, who need the love of God in the touch of kindness and concern.

Moderation characterizes their beliefs and their actions. Though socially conservative, most are theologically moderate. They are aware of justice issues, but are not naturally focused on systemic analyses of social evils. Although they do not see social problems through the lenses of "great" causes, they can take stands of conscience when they feel forced by circumstance, and can move into advocacy roles when necessary.

More naturally, servants design ministries that sustain individuals through long-term needs. These churches provide continuing help to seniors with home repairs or insurance paperwork, or help families to develop mutual support systems. Frequently they feel no need for outside assistance and are not aggressive in seeking allies in their ministries. Rather, they may form quiet, neighborly relationships with other institutions and individuals—most often churches—who can help them in helping others.

Sometimes the servant's sense of caring for others risks paternalism, creating dependency in those who are receiving help. Yet they faithfully live out the Lord's words, "I was hungry and you gave me food, thirsty and you gave me drink. . . . "

In summary, the dominant characteristics of these images among the churches in our study include the following:

*Survivor:* Is Reactive to the Crises of an Overwhelming World
  Leadership feels stretched, often near burnout.
  Uses crisis situations to generate strong support.
  Close-knit membership with highly participatory decision-making.
  Few, safe, and familiar partners.
  Theologically evangelical and moderate, socially liberal.

*Crusader:* Is Proactive to Translate Crises into Causes
  Dramatic leaders with a clarity of vision.

Strongly independent attitude, responsive to trends.
High membership participation in mission if not in decisions.
Develops functional coalitions, not long-term partners.
Theologically moderate and evangelical, but liberal and even radical on social issues.

*Pillar:* Takes Civic Responsibility That Embraces the Community
Professionally trained and organizationally supported leaders.
Larger congregations with lower sense of intimacy and more limited participation in decision-making.
Many partners, but mostly other churches.
Theologically liberal and moderate, but socially conservative.
Tends toward comprehensive, multiservice ministries.

*Pilgrim:* Cares for Extended Family or Cultural Group
Leaders with traditional values drawn from their ethnic group.
Strong sense of history, and active social ministry participation.
Few partners, mostly drawn from familiar networks.
Theologically moderate, but liberal on social issues.
Ministries that care for "our own" or "our adopted" people.

*Servant:* Provides Support for Individuals Who Need Help
Leaders who are seen as caregivers.
Low group cohesiveness, a gathering of individuals.
Few partners, mostly resources in times of specific need.
Theologically moderate, socially conservative.
Ministries of direct, personal, and limited services.

## Observations and Implications

This variety of images can free local church leaders from the mistaken idea that there is only one way to generate social ministry. There are many, and we have identified profiles of five of these approaches. In the process, what we have learned from these social ministries has called into question many of the old stereotypes about congregational limits or theological assumptions. The congregation that recognizes its own self-image can generate commitment when it claims its own style. It can build coalitions when it identifies its similarities with some churches and differences with others. To encourage these comparisons, we offer observations in four areas.

### Recognizing Allies and Developing Coalitions

Similarities draw some congregations together. Crusaders may appear—and feel—invincible, while survivors are vulnerable, struggling to stay alive. Yet congregations with these two self-images often discover a common bond in their level of energy and willingness to act. They have a natural affinity in their shared perception that social issues have systemic causes, and their Christian convictions provide a foundation for their ministries of social justice.

Crusader churches live on the active edge, while pilgrim congregations march to a steadier beat, but they share many values—the high priority they put on social ministries, their liberal orientation to social issues, and their personal motivation to work for justice causes. Crusaders, pilgrims, and survivors are often allies—and sometimes the images overlap.

Differences can be the basis for coalitions in ministry, especially when churches discover how much they need each other's strengths. Servants and crusaders begin at opposite ends of the social justice scale—servants by helping individuals, and crusaders by challenging systems. When an inner-city servant church realized the need for transitional housing for homeless people in their community, they formed a powerful alliance with a crusader church from the university district across town. The two churches have very different histories, theological orientations, and personal gifts. What unites them is their shared vision of a better, more caring community—and their teamwork is amazingly effective.

Pillars and survivors are polar opposites in everything from bank accounts to self-confidence; but when they work together, they have an impact on the community and on each other. We have seen one struggling congregation in a depressed area of a midwestern city build a remarkable partnership with a large metropolitan congregation on the outskirts. The survivor church receives resources without losing its autonomy, and the pillar church has found a place to focus its volunteers and other resources in mission. Both are grateful for opportunities to share.

Effective social ministry begins with self-awareness—not only for the greater health and growth of a single congregation, but also to enable the cooperation of those who know who they are and what they bring to a unity forged in a common task.

### Faith—Yes! Theology—No!

Familiar theological models suggest that liberal churches are more likely to be activist in social issues and social ministries, while evangelical congregations (with an emphasis on personal salvation and the Bible as the literal word of God) are more apt to withdraw from engagement in social issues or social ministries.[3] Members in our project churches saw their ministries as expressions of their Christian faith, but not according to the familiar assumptions about theological foundations for social ministry.

The most active congregations, crusaders and survivors, are not motivated by liberal theological perspectives. Their strong commitments to social ministry were more likely to have moderate or evangelical theological roots. We can only speculate that liberal churches may be more shaped by class differences, or more divided by the pluralism they embrace, while evangelical churches are more willing to be unified, decisive, and forceful. The majority of crusader churches are inclined to embrace both the salvation of souls and a passion for social justice. One urban congregation emphasizes personal evangelism with preaching for decision and an altar call, then follows with a week full of programs responding to the needs of battered women and single-parent families, and to the hope for developing low-cost shelter for these community residents.

Liberal theology appears more consistently in the pillar churches, but these congregations are conservative on social issues and relatively unaware of the social justice dimensions of ministry. Servant churches, who care the most about helping individuals, have moderate doctrinal commitments and the least interest in the systemic causes of social problems. One tall-steeple church with traditional liturgy, solid preaching, and a friendly, homogeneous membership has responded to the needs of the unemployed with a careful, well-documented plan to provide help for hurting people— but does not make waves either in the church or in the community.

Throughout our study, motivations for social ministry have not been associated with any particular theological stance or doctrine. Rather, the appeal to work for social ministries and to advocate for justice is nurtured by a more universal community concern and affinity with human need, and is supported by a broad-based Christian faith that finds roots in the full spectrum of theological beliefs.

## Agents of Change

Clout—the ability to make a difference—appears in surprising places. The tall steeples of pillar churches command respect, and the dramatic issues of crusaders demand attention. But even a survivor church may well have more strength for ministry than it realizes. Survivor congregations can use their crises as resources for attacking their sense of being overwhelmed by forces beyond their control. When they objectify and lift up those crises, they can mobilize a deep and persistent commitment to meet the challenges.

One small congregation that has struggled to survive because of its size (thirty-five members) has used its location on the tense boundary between a low-income neighborhood and a more affluent university enclave to mobilize people from both communities in an educational program for youth. Their program, new and small but lively, has generated a sense of pride and satisfaction in participants from both neighborhoods, strengthened the commitments of the congregation, and surprised them with new recognition in denominational circles. In this way some congregations develop a larger dream in which they become agents for change far beyond their size or individual resources.

Pilgrims are also apt to underestimate their power to change communities through social ministries. Pilgrim churches frequently have had little experience as agents of community change. Although they may have a cherished history and wide community contacts, they may never have recognized or made use of their status as respected community institutions. One rural church has used latent pride in the community's history to rally dispirited neighbors to work together again. A black congregation became so incensed about children loitering in betting parlors at the rear of convenience stores that they mobilized their network of family, friends, colleagues, and neighborhood contacts to help them create alternative activities for youth of the area. Working in programs of social ministry and issues of social justice has given fresh affirmation to pilgrim congregations and has encouraged them to flex their community muscles in new and creative ways.

### Unique Gifts

Each self-image has special, irreplaceable gifts that these congregations alone can offer to others through social ministry, gifts that make them stronger and richer in the act of giving:

The survivors can cope where other styles would collapse.
The crusaders can raise issues where others might let them slide.
The pillars can legitimate change where others might ignore it.
The pilgrims can embrace diversity where others might deny it.
The servants can care for individuals who might otherwise be lost.

Ministering congregations are strengthened by translating their faith into action, and the community gains from them all. There is no single way to engage in social ministry—thank God!

## NOTES

1. For an expanded discussion of some biblical and contemporary self-images, see Carl S. Dudley, "Using Church Images for Commitment, Conflict, and Renewal," in C. Ellis Nelson, *Congregations: Their Power to Form and Transform* (Atlanta: John Knox Press, 1988), pp. 89–113.

2. For the historical sources used by congregations in developing these images, see Carl S. Dudley, "Saints, Crises, and Other Memories That Energize the Church," keynote address to SCUPE Urban Congress, Chicago, April 13, 1988. Reprinted in *Action Information* (Washington, D.C.: Alban Institute), January-February and March-April 1989.

3. Although this position has been frequently articulated, its most recent, careful, and well-documented statement can be found in the work by David A. Roozen, William J. McKinney, and Jackson W. Carroll, *Varieties of Religious Presence* (New York: Pilgrim Press, 1984).

# PART TWO

# Strategies

# SEVEN

# Preserving Christian Identity: The Task of Leadership in the Congregation

## JACKSON W. CARROLL

There has been growing recognition that congregations, like individuals, have identities. In the *Handbook for Congregational Studies* (Carroll, Dudley, and McKinney, 1986:21), my colleagues and I define a congregation's identity as "the persistent set of beliefs, values, patterns, symbols, stories, and style that makes a congregation distinctive." We believe that over time each congregation develops its own identity, its own way of being a congregation. Its identity is shaped by its heritage, its context, and the characteristics of its members.[1]

Several authors in this volume discuss aspects of congregational identity or culture (a broader concept that includes identity). They emphasize that leaders need to know and respect their congregation's distinctive identity if they are to lead effectively.

There is a temptation, however, to focus only on aspects of a congregation's identity that derive from its particular history, its people, or its size and location. These are important, but they are only part of the picture.

Even as each congregation has a distinctive identity, each is also a particular embodiment of the body of Christ. Thus, insofar as a congregation is faithful to its calling to be the church, its particular identity is also an expression of a *Christian* identity. This does not imply sameness. The various contributors to identity—history, size, location, member characteristics—preclude sameness. It does, however, imply that congregational leaders give constant attention to the congregation's faithfulness to its calling as the body of Christ as it expresses this calling in the particularities of its heritage, time, and place.

In this chapter, I propose a way of understanding this key leadership task, especially for clergy. I consider three broad leadership functions: meaning interpretation, community formation, and support of the congregation's public ministry.[2]

125

The three leadership functions are interrelated ways of describing the single task of preserving Christian identity. I find it helpful to think of them as facets of a cut diamond. There is only one stone, but it has different sides from which it can be viewed. While each facet reflects a peculiar angle on the one stone, it is not separable from the whole. It participates in it fully. Similarly, each of the three leadership functions provides a different but interdependent angle on the one core task of ministry. We can consider these functions separately, but in the life of the congregation they cannot be pulled apart, as I shall try to describe.

These ways of characterizing clergy leadership are important because they help us make new connections and see new possibilities that traditional role descriptions—which often appear to be discrete, unrelated tasks—may obscure. I will describe each of the three facets and then present an extended example to illustrate their meaning and interdependence.

## Meaning Interpretation

First, there is the clergy's function as *interpreter of meaning*. Much of what a pastor does in specific pastoral roles—preaching, designing and leading the liturgy, teaching, counseling, and organizational leadership—is aimed at assisting others to reflect on and interpret their personal and social experiences in the light of God's purposes in Jesus Christ.

As individuals, we face hopes, fears, disappointments, moral dilemmas, life changes, and life crises that confront us with questions of meaning, often raising the issue of the ultimate meaningfulness of life. Transition points—puberty, marriage, childbirth, divorce, retirement, death—are particularly challenging moments that threaten to rip the fabric of meaning by introducing new and often unanticipated experiences.

Congregations, too, experience crises of meaning: decisions about the future, conflicts over particular programs, dilemmas over how to spend limited resources, interpersonal or intergroup conflicts, and many other such issues that call for reflection, interpretation, and decision.

The pastoral task is that of standing with individuals or the congregation as a corporate body in these experiences, helping them to face them and give meaning to them in the light of the gospel. The pastor helps members reflect on these experiences, framing or reframing them in terms of the gospel and exploring responses to them in ways that express their Christian identity. Expressed slightly differently, the task is to break open the symbols of the tradition in such a way that they illumine the concrete and sometimes threatening issues of life—personal and social—in fresh and helpful ways.

The apostle Paul provides an example: For the early Christian community, Jesus' death on the cross was a radically disturbing experience. It created what social psychologists (e.g., Festinger, 1957) call "cognitive dissonance." Cognitive dissonance is a crisis of meaning that arises when one's expectations or beliefs are challenged by objective events or by other beliefs that appear contradictory. Two powerful examples of meaning interpretation are Paul's reinterpretation (reframing) of the cross as the foolishness and weakness of God that is wiser and more powerful than the world (1 Cor. 1:25) and his use of the cross-resurrection theme as the central symbol of Christians' experience. They enabled the early Christians to celebrate the foolishness of the cross and reframe their own life experiences in terms of Jesus' death and resurrection in ways that energized them for mission.[3]

Today we face a genuine difficulty: Many people find the teachings and symbols of faith opaque, out of touch with their experiences. As Presbyterian pastor Wallace Alston (1970) expressed it pungently: "The Christian community has allowed its language of faith to die without benefit of resurrection." What we need, he continues, is

> ministers who are willing to stay in a conflict-ridden local parish and to struggle for a vital language of faith that is both faithful to the tradition of the Church and historical for the contemporary moment. We need ministers, in other words, who are willing to shun the temptation to be amateur psychiatrists or amateur sociologists and dare to do what they were trained and ordained to do, namely, to be theologians in the context of a local community of faith.

We have gone through a period of deemphasis of the pastor's role as meaning interpreter or theologian in the congregation. Theological educators complain that students are electing practical courses in the curriculum and neglecting foundational courses that undergird practice. At the same time, some seminaries have contributed to the deemphasis of meaning interpretation by making courses in homiletics optional. Moreover, recent accents in clergy continuing education seem to have been more often on issues of organizational development and conflict management (important issues, to be sure) than on the clergy's interpretive roles, including developing the capacity to think theologically about parish management.

Meanwhile laity continue to send signals about their longing for help in discerning the meaning of the faith for their lives. In parish survey after parish survey, members express their greatest hope (along with dissatisfaction due to unfulfilled hopes) that their church will assist them in "deepening their spiritual life." In a recent national survey, Catholic and Protestant parish lay leaders expressed similar disappointment with their current clergy leadership on the same issue (Hoge, Carroll, and Scheets, 1989). The phrase "deepening their spiritual life" may mean a number of things, but I believe that at heart it conveys an expectation by laity that their pastor will help them to connect their own stories—personal and parish—to the stories and symbols of the Christian faith in a way that gives meaning and direction to their lives. In other words, they want pastors who are the kind of theologians in the congregation that Alston describes.

In the worship services of the church that our family attends, we symbolize this expectation by the practice, derived from early New England church life, of having a lay person take the Bible from the communion table to the pulpit and present it to the pastor at the time for the lessons and sermon. Following the sermon, the pastor returns the Bible to the congregation, putting it back on the table. In this act, we ask the pastor to interpret the word—break open the tradition as the bread is broken in the eucharist—in such a way that it helps us to make sense of our experiences. Returning it to us reminds us of our responsibility to live out of that word as we scatter from the worship service to the various settings where we are called to be in ministry. Neither pastor nor congregation always succeeds in living up to the expectations of the ritual act. Nonetheless, it is a potent reminder, Sunday after Sunday, of what we expect of each other.

While meaning interpretation sounds as if it were primarily a verbal, cognitive enterprise, it is considerably more. Much in our lives occurs at a nondiscursive level—things that we can feel, see, smell, hear and do, but which we find difficult if not impossible to put into words or concepts. When a questioner asked Anna Pavlova, "What do you say when you dance?" she is said to have responded, "If I could tell you, I wouldn't dance." Reflecting on Pavlova's comment, Orrin Klapp (1969: 19–20) refers to this and other nondiscursive modes of communication as "mystique." It is the whole meaning that a person gets without being able to describe it verbally or conceptually. Much of the meaning interpretation in which the church engages has this nondiscursive character. Through the liturgy, in music, in the sacraments, in symbols of the worship space, in priorities symbolized in the church budget, in the coffee and donuts of the fellowship hour, in a silent presence with a family at a time of bereavement, we communicate meanings that we cannot always put into words.

## Community Formation

The church is not only a place where we are helped to give meaning to our lives. It is also a community of belonging in which individuals are called out of their loneliness and isolation into caring, supportive relationships with others who share a commitment to Jesus Christ. It is a community where members are nurtured in the virtues of Christian life. Through the quality of its community life the church bears witness to the meaning of justice and reconciliation as marks of God's coming reign which is both present now and yet to come. This requires a second leadership task: *community formation*, helping to shape the congregation as a community of belonging.

There is a close relationship between this task and meaning interpretation. Each task reinforces the other in the service of preserving Christian identity. Telling the gospel story helps to define the character and contours of Christian community. Participation in a community that offers fellowship, expresses caring and support, and seeks justice in the relationships of its members is an eloquent example in action of the meaning of the gospel story. Conversely, even the most persuasive telling of the gospel story will have difficulty overcoming the negative witness of a mean-spirited, unjust community.

Building vital Christian community is essential to maintaining Christian identity in yet another way. Primary communities such as the church are examples of what Peter Berger and Thomas Luckmann (1966) have called "plausibility structures." In these communities, the plausibility or believability of a particular understanding of reality is sustained through conversation and through various symbolic and ritual expressions. As Berger (1967: 46–47) has written, "*All* religious traditions, irrespective of their several 'ecclesiologies' or lack of same, require specific communities for their continuing plausibility." This, he suggests, is one general meaning of the maxim "Outside the church there is no salvation." When there are weak plausibility structures, so also "the Christian world begins to totter and its reality ceases to impose itself [to the individual] as self-evident truth. . . . The firmer the plausibility structure is, the firmer will be the world that is (based) upon it." Put another way, the more powerful the experience of belonging to a congregation, the more plausible and vital will be its interpretation of the Christian story.

For all these reasons, the belonging dimension of the church is not an option. Community formation is a primary leadership task with pastors working to form and sustain the relationships and structures of the gathered community and helping it maintain its identity as the body of Christ. As the author of Ephesians expressed it, the aim is "building up the body of Christ, until we all attain to the unity of the faith and of the knowledge of the Son of God . . . to the measure of the stature of the fulness of Christ" (Eph. 4:12–13).

One element of the clergy's community formation role is as celebrant of the sacraments, incorporating individuals into the family of God in baptism, bringing people together around the table in the eucharist. There is an obvious overlap with the interpretive role that I described above, especially with some of its nondiscursive elements.

Biblical scholar Wayne Meeks (1982) demonstrates this connection in his fascinating analysis of Pauline congregations, using the tools of sociology. Paul's interpretation of baptism and eucharist created powerful symbolic means of community formation, as well as meaning interpretation in the face of cognitive dissonance. Those who were converts to the churches were a disparate group: people of means (especially wealthy women), artisans, tradesmen, masters and slaves. If they shared anything in common, it was discrepant statuses—statuses that were partly valued, partly devalued in the social world of the first century. Their rituals—especially baptism and eucharist—provided powerful, mostly nonverbal symbols of participation in a new reality and a new community. Entrants into the community died to the old statuses that defined them in society and were raised to a new sense of personhood in fellowship with Christ and with each other. They participated in a new interpretation of their lives and a new community. Baptism symbolized this nonverbally as new entrants experienced the drama of being stripped of their old identity (often literally by shedding their clothes), cleansed of the past, and raised to new relationship with Christ and one another. The Lord's Supper, with its sharing together in Christ's death and resurrection, incorporated them into a new community, promoted solidarity, and helped them define a distinctive Christian identity.

These sacraments continue to be central, nondiscursive means for shaping Christian identity: baptism as the event that incorporates us into God's family and gives us our vocation to ministry as God's people; eucharist as the continuing renewal of communion with Christ and one another in God's family and as a reminder that our Christian identity is expressed in a servant ministry of life broken and poured out for others. These and other liturgical actions are central to the clergy's role in community formation.

Community formation also requires theological and sociological insight into the nature and functioning of communities and the skills of a midwife in assisting the community into being: the ability to understand congregations and their dynamics, managerial and administrative skills, skills in group relationships and conflict management, political and persuasive skills. Its aim is a community life whose structures and processes are faithful to its identity as the body of Christ and also appropriate to the concrete situation in which the congregation finds itself—its size, its resources, its setting.

In spite of what I said earlier about the growing emphasis on organizational development and conflict management in clergy continuing-education opportunities, neither clergy nor theological educators always view the managerial and administrative aspects of community building as particularly important or having theological undergirding.[4] When H. Richard Niebuhr (1956) proposed "pastoral director" as an appropriate image of ordained ministry, he was criticized for lending credence to what seemed to be a "big operator," management-oriented, nontheological view of ordained ministry—what some have referred to as the manager model of ministry (Hough and Cobb, 1986). Pastoral director may have suggested this, but it was clearly not what Niebuhr intended. Instead, he derived his image from the monastic tradition and intended by it leadership in community formation and maintenance. Such a role, as Niebuhr pointed out, not only continues to be of central importance to the church but has historic links with the early church's role of bishop or *episcopos*, who functioned as overseer of one or more congregations, presiding at the eucharist and giving pastoral guidance (including administration) to the gathered life of the community. The church continues to require such leadership as a means of preserving its Christian identity under changing circumstances.

## Empowering Public Ministry

The third pastoral task reflects the role of the church as a community of empowerment. The aim is empowering members, collectively and individually, to live as the people of God in the world.

This pastoral task is analogous to a role that community development workers have created in Haiti. They train leaders whom they call *animateurs*, men and women who learn group formation and mobilization techniques to help others in their groups respond constructively to their situations. *Animateurs* are trained to help their groups analyze their problems, explore solutions, and develop ways to implement them. As one author (Hollar, 1988) described the goal, "The key is to 'animate groups to think and act for themselves, not to dictate decisions from outside.' " I believe that a similar role is required of clergy who become *animateurs* of their congregations with respect to their corporate and individual ministries beyond the walls of the church.

This is no simple or easy task. It has become increasingly difficult for Christians to speak with the language of faith or to act in accord with their Christian identity in secular social settings. A secular society, such as the one in which we live, attempts to render public expressions of faith, either in language or behavior, as at best *mere* personal opinion and at worst in bad taste. It is therefore no mean task for clergy and laity to discover ways of asserting the power and relevance of their faith in contexts that generally exclude the relevance of religious speech and behavior. Sometimes this requires bold and explicit profession of one's faith and its implications. No other way seems defensible. At the same time, I believe that we are also called to accompany our witness with a willingness to remain in dialogue with other perspectives and a humility that prevents us from claiming to have a direct line to God.

Often, however, what is called for is adopting what Dietrich Bonhoeffer (1955:84ff.) called a "penultimate" rather than an "ultimate" attitude. This means forgoing speech or actions that explicitly express one's ultimate faith convictions. It involves instead finding penultimate ways of living out of one's faith convictions, ways of speaking and acting that respect the everyday reality that we share with others in the situation who may not hold our ultimate convictions. It involves finding common ground with them on which to work for the common good: more humane, fair, or just solutions to issues at work, in the community, or in the nation. Bonhoeffer asks:

> Does one not in some cases, by remaining deliberately in the penultimate, perhaps point all the more genuinely to the ultimate, which God will speak in His own time? . . . Does not this mean that, over and over again, the penultimate will be what commends itself precisely for the sake of the ultimate, and that it will have to be done not with a heavy conscience but with a clear one?

One can argue that the role of empowerment really derives from the meaning interpretation and community formation roles. If the pastor's role as interpreter of meaning includes helping laity to explore their calling in terms of concrete issues of family, work, or public life, then the pastor is already engaged in the empowering role. Similarly, if pastors are helping to form a community in the church where individuals find healing, renewal, and support and are nurtured in the virtues of the Christian life, they are also engaged in supporting the public ministries of these persons.

Empowering public ministry warrants emphasis as a distinctive task for two reasons. One is the ease with which we come to subsume the meaning of the church in terms of its gathered life. Emphasizing the task of supporting public ministry focuses attention on the life of the people of God in the world as the primary arena for ministry. Secondly, clergy too belong to the *laos*, God's people in the world. In spite of the priority attention that clergy must give to the gathered life of the church, they have vital and important roles in the broader community, modeling what it means to live as Christians in public life and acting as symbolic representatives of religion in public affairs. I do not advocate either the restriction of the clergy role to the internal life of the church, a nineteenth-century invention, or the view, so pervasive today, that limits the congregation's role (clergy and laity) to the private sphere.

Several years ago two colleagues and I studied the relation of religion to public life in Hartford, Connecticut (McKinney, Roozen, and Carroll, 1982; Roozen, McKinney, and Carroll, 1984). A primary finding was the importance of pastoral leadership for shaping how a congregation related to public life, whether this relationship was interpreted as winning converts, providing service, or social action. How pastors defined and interpreted the congregation's role in public life, on the one hand, and how they modeled that role in their own involvement in the life of the community, on the other, were crucial to the congregation's orientation and involvement (or lack thereof) in public life. Additionally, we found that community leaders tended to identify religion with religious professionals. Unless ministers, priests, or rabbis were themselves visible in public affairs, religion itself was often viewed as absent.

There are clearly problems with such a view from the perspective of shared ministry. It is laity who are daily inhabitants of the institutions of the public world and whose primary calling is to exercise their ministries in these institutions. Clergy, nevertheless, play a crucial role in this arena. Beyond their symbolic role as institutional representatives of religion, they need also to bring expertise to the church–social context interface. This includes the capacity to analyze community dynamics and public issues, an understanding of both the penultimate character of issues and their relation to the Christian story, and a willingness to engage with others (inside and outside the church) in reflection and action on the issues.

## Putting It Together: An Example

Earlier I described the three core tasks as similar to facets of a single stone—each distinct but also part of a whole that cannot, in last analysis, be treated independently. The meanings associated with Christian identity help to give belonging a focus and purpose. We do not belong for belonging's sake; we belong to the community of Jesus Christ. Belonging, in turn, provides the context—the plausibility structures—whereby the meanings are explored, rehearsed, and sustained in mutual conversation and ritual behavior. Both meaning and belonging are, in turn, essential for empowering the church's ministry in public life. And attempting to live out of a Christian identity in public life raises new questions of meaning and makes us aware of our need of a supportive and sustaining community. The interdependence of the three tasks can be seen in the following extended example.[5]

Colchester Federated Church (United Church of Christ and American Baptist) is a congregation of approximately six hundred members located in what until recently was a small Connecticut town that had not been much affected by urban growth. In the mid-1970s, the members were primarily farmers, clerical and production workers, and small-business people. They were faithful and loyal, but unaccustomed to thinking in new ways about their church's mission. By the 1980s, however, the town and congregation had experienced a growth spurt with younger, more professionally educated workers moving in and joining the church. They brought new ideas and created a leaven for change. In 1980 the church called a new pastor, the Rev. Davida Foy Crabtree. Under her leadership the church has grown in membership and member involvement. More important, the church has also grown in the way it expresses its corporate life and mission.

When she came to the church, the pastor was committed to a vision of the ministry of the laity—drawn from the larger Christian tradition—that became the guiding image for much of her work in pastoral care and organizational leadership. While she found some laity in the congregation who affirmed this vision, it was not really shared by the majority of members, except perhaps in the perfunctory way that many Protestants express belief in the "priesthood of all believers." The vision was part of the congregation's broader Christian identity, but it was not an operational part of the local culture of the congregation, which tended to restrict ministry to the ordained leader.

Initially, she expressed her vision primarily in preaching and in teaching opportunities that she initiated—for example, an adult retreat on "Discovering Our Gifts" and a conference focused on the theme "Beyond a Sunday Christianity." During this time, the leadership also began a planning process—the congregation's first experience with formal planning—and the pastor entered a doctor of ministry program intent on making shared ministry the focus of her work.

A major breakthrough in developing greater ownership of the shared ministry emphasis came in 1986 with the recognition that retreats and conferences were familiar ways of working to college educated, middle-class managers and professionals, but they were somewhat alien to less verbally skilled working-class people. Therefore, she formed a listening team of three laity (a machinist, an executive, and a data-base analyst), who invited occupational groups to spend an evening talking about their work. The pastor served as a silent observer-recorder. The people—teachers, office and production workers—were encouraged to talk about their satisfactions and frustrations, and they were asked a question that invariably stymied them: "Does it make any difference that you are a Christian on your job?" Despite the difficulty, feedback indicated that the experience was a positive one, and some wanted to go further.

A next step was creation of a covenant group of twelve members who spent ten months together considering issues of faith and work, with both the pastor and a new associate pastor participating—symbolic of the importance that both clergy attached to the emphasis. Through various ways—Bible study, case studies of work situations, reading, and sharing work experiences—group members developed a capacity to think and talk about their faith and its relation to their work and other aspects of their lives, a new experience for most of them. For example, the somewhat esoteric biblical concepts of "principalities and powers" came alive for them as they explored the ways that institutional aspects of the work situation and church practice seem to have a life of their own and often seem to hold people in bondage. So too did the meaning of Christ as liberator—a central image of the pastor's theology—take on new importance. Members also experienced significant caring and support from others in the group.

They encouraged and held each other accountable in the exercise of their ministries in daily life. Subsequently, other covenant groups were formed along the lines of the first one.

Various ways of including the broader congregation in the covenant groups' work were used, including additional conferences and retreats. With the groups' assistance, the pastors began to include a special vocation prayer in the Sunday worship. Members provided suggestions from their work experience to help shape the prayers. A different occupation was featured each week with a visual reminder of the work placed on the communion table before the cross. A prayer was said for all in that occupation. For example, when electricians were the focus, coils of wire and some tools were placed on the table and the following prayer was used:

> Creator God, you are the source of all energy and power. We bring before you this day those who work with the power of electricity, who seek to channel, transform and convert a dangerous energy into power for good. Guard them and keep them safe. Give them patience with tracking problems to their source, and caution in their work. And grant them a sense of ministry in their making our lives safe, in their striving for excellence, in their dealings with people. In the name of Jesus, Amen.

Meanwhile, as part of a course assignment, the pastor "shadowed" several members of her congregation at their work—that is, she shared a workday with them, observing their on-the-job experiences. She found that this opened significant new opportunities for pastoral care, and now she regularly meets parishioners for lunch at their work settings.

As the emphasis on ministry in the workplace progressed, the pastor and some of her leaders became aware of a deeper issue that had to be addressed if it was to take hold in a significant and lasting way: The structure of the congregation itself had to be addressed. As presently organized, the congregation is what she calls a "come" structure. It is concerned primarily with bringing members to the church building to participate in and support its gathered life. It is not a "go out" structure that also supports and encourages ministry in the church's scattered life. As she sees it (Crabtree, 1989:11), "If a congregation is serious about supporting its members in discerning and living out their ministries, it must be prepared to incarnate that support in the systems of its life." To initiate this kind of reflection, she developed a group of questions for each board and committee, inviting them to consider how their work might be recast to empower the ministry of the laity both within the congregation and, especially, beyond it. She began to shape the outlines of what she called a "management system" to structure the church so that it would more effectively empower lay ministry. Sharing this with the diaconate, reinforced by discussions with them on the meaning of ministry, led to the creation of a special short-term task force to develop a plan for restructuring the congregation as a "go out" structure under the diaconate's leadership. That process is currently underway with indications that a growing number of lay leaders and members have come to share their pastor's vision. At the same time, they are sensitive to those members who have not yet caught the vision and who look to the church with more traditional expectations. They are concerned that these people not feel neglected or excluded from the church's ministry.

This is an exciting and encouraging story, only a part of which I have been able to tell here. It is also an ongoing story. A real test will come in the congregation's ability to sustain and grow in its emphasis on shared ministry, with or without its current pastor. My major reason for telling the story, however, is as a clear example of the interrelationship and interdependence of the three core tasks of ministry.

The pastor's initial focus was on the third task, encouraging and supporting the laity's public ministry, especially in their work life. That was reinforced by preaching and teaching—meaning interpretation—in which she tried to help members understand their vocation to ministry. Later, too, the members' vocation to ministry became part of the liturgy and symbols in the vocation prayers. Had she stopped with the interpretive task, however, it is unlikely that her vision would have taken hold in the consciousness of members. In addition to the worship services, the covenant group experience provided an important "plausibility structure" and center for belonging where faith and everyday experience could be talked about frankly in a supportive, caring environment. The groups also took on the character of "accountability" as well as plausibility structures, where people not only talk about their convictions but hold one another accountable for living by them. Even more was needed, however, if the vision was to take shape and become incarnate as part of the congregation's identity and character: it had to become part of the institutional fabric—thus the emphasis on the management system that is still under way in the church. How that restructuring takes shape and whether it can overcome years of doing things "the way we've always done them" remains to be seen. It is, however, a crucial aspect of community building, which leaders must undertake if the congregation is to embody its vision.

I wish to emphasize that I do not intend this as an example that other congregations should attempt to duplicate. For many congregations the particular expression of their vision may be different, dictated by the way they understand their calling to live out a Christian identity in their distinctive culture and context. Yet, however they give expression to their vision of what it means for them to be the church, it will need to be interpreted in preaching and teaching and celebrated liturgically so that members can understand their own experiences and stories in its light. It must also be sustained in a community where it becomes real through conversation, sharing, and support and where the community is structured in such a way as to incarnate the vision. And members need support and a sense of accountability to live out of the vision, individually and corporately, in the church's scattered life. These things will not happen without strong leadership, especially that of clergy who function as meaning interpreters, community builders, and enablers of public ministry.


NOTES

1. This chapter is adapted from the author's forthcoming book *As One with Authority: Reflective Leadership in Ministry*, which grows out of extensive observation of congregational life and reflection with clergy and laity on their ministries. Time for research and writing was made possible by a grant from the Lilly Endowment.

2. This functional way of construing the church builds on a sociological interpretation of religion that describes religion's functions or consequences as providing meaning and belonging to individual participants and groups. See McGuire (1987:23ff.). I add a third function, empowerment, which is actually derivative of the experience of meaning and belonging.

3. For an extended discussion of cognitive dissonance in relation to the first Christians, see Gager (1975) and Dudley and Hilgert (1987).

4. This was a primary finding of Samuel Blizzard's (1985) research on ministerial roles. While the original research was conducted in the 1950s, there is little evidence that the situation has changed appreciably since that time.

5. The example comes from a doctor of ministry project report, subsequently published (Crabtree, 1989).


WORKS CITED

Alston, Wallace M., Jr.
        1970          "The Minister as Theologian." Lecture presented at a Duke
                      Divinity School seminar in Columbia, S.C.

Berger, Peter L.
    1967        *The Sacred Canopy*. Garden City, N.Y.: Doubleday & Co.

Berger, Peter L., and Thomas Luckmann
    1966        *The Social Construction of Reality*. Garden City, N.Y.: Double-
                day & Co.

Blizzard, Samuel W.
    1985        *The Protestant Parish Minister*. Washington, D.C.: Society for
                the Scientific Study of Religion.

Bonhoeffer, Dietrich
    1955        *Ethics*. Edited by Eberhard Bethge. New York: Macmillan Co.

Carroll, Jackson W., Carl S. Dudley, and William McKinney
    1986        *Handbook for Congregational Studies*. Nashville: Abingdon
                Press.

Crabtree, Davida Foy
    1989        *The Empowering Church*. Washington, D.C.: Alban Institute.

Dudley, Carl S., and Earl Hilgert
    1987        *New Testament Tensions and the Contemporary Church*. Phila-
                delphia: Fortress Press.

Festinger, Leon
    1957        *A Theory of Cognitive Dissonance*. Stanford, Calif.: Stanford
                University Press.

Gager, John G.
    1975        *Kingdom and Community*. Englewood Cliffs, N.J.: Prentice-
                Hall.

Hoge, Dean R., Jackson W. Carroll, and Francis K. Scheets
    1989        *Patterns of Parish Leadership*. Kansas City, Mo.: Sheed &
                Ward.

Hollar, Larry
    1988        "Haiti: A People's Struggle for Hope." *Bread for the World
                Background Papers*, no. 107 (September).

Hough, Joseph C., Jr., and John B. Cobb, Jr.
    1986        *Christian Identity and Theological Education*. Atlanta: Schol-
                ars Press.

Klapp, Orrin
    1969        *Collective Search for Identity*. New York: Holt, Rinehart &
                Winston.

McGuire, Meredith B.
    1987        *Religion: The Social Context*. 2nd edition. Belmont, Calif.:
                Wadsworth Publishing Co.

McKinney, William, David A. Roozen, and Jackson W. Carroll
    1982        *Religion's Public Presence*. Washington: Alban Institute.

Meeks, Wayne A.
  1982        *The First Urban Christians: The Social World of the Apostle Paul.* New Haven, Conn.: Yale University Press.

Niebuhr, H. Richard, et al.
  1956        *The Purpose of the Church and Its Ministry.* New York: Harper & Brothers.

Roozen, David A., William McKinney, and Jackson W. Carroll
  1984        *Varieties of Religious Presence.* New York: Pilgrim Press.

# EIGHT

# Leading from Within

## DOUGLAS ALAN WALRATH

In this chapter I want to share some reflections and then some suggestions about leadership in small congregations.[1] My thinking draws heavily
on insights that pastors and lay leaders of rural, small churches shared
during two surveys conducted by the Small Church Leadership Program at
Bangor Theological Seminary (Walrath and Walrath, 1988; 1989). While
the focus of the chapter is on the issues outsiders face when they become
pastors within rural, small churches, I believe those who are seeking to
become established leaders within any culture different from their own
native culture will find the insights and suggestions in the chapter helpful.

## Urban Norms and Rural Ministry

Most of us who are pastors strive to shape our ministries according to
biblical and theological norms. However, as we do so we may be more
affected by cultural norms than most of us realize or would like to admit.
My research during the past three years indicates that such cultural shaping can become painfully apparent when pastors acculturated into the
urban culture that now dominates mainline U.S. denominations become
leaders of rural, small congregations. Especially those who continue to hold
to some of the most widely accepted cultural models of church and ministry
often discover that urban acculturation limits their ability to minister with
rural, small congregations.

For example, one cultural model of the church that seems to enjoy wide
popularity today is what I call the "organizational/programmatic" model.
According to this model a "good" congregation is one that is organizationally and programmatically effective. Its program contains varied offerings
designed to address the range of needs and interests of its members and
others the congregation hopes to attract. Efficient organization, staff, and

141

facilities support the church's program. In the view of those who hold this model up as a norm, an effective organizational/programmatic congregation can be expected to grow in numbers as it refines and expands its program to appeal to those within and around it. Vital faith is assumed to be engaging and appealing. Thus faith, appealing program, and organizational effectiveness are interconnected as elements of the model: a congregation that is organizationally and programmatically effective can be expected to become a large, growing church composed of Christians with vital faith.

Advocates of this organizational/programmatic model appeal to an impressive array of biblical, theological, and historical sources for support (Wagner, 1984). Reading through their arguments, however, it is equally impressive how rarely they seem prepared to recognize the degree to which cultural norms shape their thinking.

Consider, for example, the current cultural norm "Bigger is better." This norm appears to be based on two interrelated beliefs: that whatever enterprise one is engaged in (1) can be done better on a larger rather than a smaller scale, and (2) will likely become bigger if it is done better. Support for this norm seems widespread among leaders in a variety of institutions. One finds it honored among those who guide corporations and educational institutions as often as among those who lead churches. Large corporations, schools, and churches alike are held up as examples of the desired result of organizational and program effectiveness and efficiency. Contemporary books written to guide corporate leaders and church leaders are remarkably similar in perspective: Successful leaders facilitate the growth of the organizations they guide (Peters and Waterman, 1985; Callahan, 1983).

Church leaders whose thinking is shaped by this cultural faith that connects leadership effectiveness with church growth often appear to overlook, or at least play down, potentially troublesome biblical and historical evidence that churches that do not grow in numbers can be as effective as those that do. In fact, there is convincing evidence that church vitality is at least as likely to be found in small churches as it is in large (Morton, 1956; 1951; O'Connor, 1963; Schutz, 1962; Kimber, 1987). Perhaps the discounting occurs because those who are influenced by the cultural standard "Bigger is better" *assume* that small churches are not as impressive (effective, faithful) as large churches.

Another popular cultural model defines the effective minister. According to this model the ideal clergyperson is viewed as a disciplined professional who gains and maintains high levels of theoretical and practical competence. While clergy differ from other professionals in important ways, well-prepared and accomplished clergy deserve respect similar to that afforded physicians and attorneys (Hough and Cobb, 1985).

I believe this currently popular model of ministry is not only theologically questionable, it may even encourage a hazardous self-identity in some clergy, especially those who become leaders in small, rural congregations. Assigning a professional role to ministers implies that they, like physicians, have specialized knowledge that is beyond the attainment of ordinary lay people, and that much, even most, of what they do ordinary people cannot do as well, or at all. Depending on the accepted view of religious authorities in a given culture or subculture, the role that those who are termed "religious professionals" can play is defined more widely or narrowly. The role of clergy can be restricted to clearly specialized functions like celebrating the eucharist or facilitating *holy* matrimony. Or the clergyperson's role can embrace more general functions, like being identified as the authority who can define proper roles for husbands and wives, or who can define proper sex attitudes and practices for adolescents. In contemporary American society, the role of clergy tends to be defined more narrowly in urban locations and among upper-status persons, and more widely in rural locations and among lower-status groups (Merton, 1968, esp. part 2).

Professionals also are usually afforded high status. Those with superior knowledge and skill in a discipline that deals with basic matters of human life usually are given the highest status. Thus, social prerogatives accompany professional role and status. As a result, many ordinary people defer to professionals.

I believe that the hazard of encouraging a high-status, professional identity among clergy most often becomes apparent in contexts where clergy believe their special knowledge is comprehensive and superior when in fact it is not. In other words, there can be problems when clergy are captives of inappropriate cultural models and see themselves as professionals with wide-ranging authority.

When clergy, albeit unwittingly, experience their perspectives as superior, and when they are *not* natives of or integrated within the culture where they are practicing ministry, they may advocate beliefs and prescribe practices that are not helpful, that in fact may even be damaging, to those among whom they minister. The history of missions abounds with discussions of this dilemma, most ably summarized in William R. Hutchinson's book *Errand to the World: American Protestant Thought and For-*

*eign Missions* (1987; see also Walrath, 1988). Missionaries who seek to
share their faith and experience themselves as culturally superior may
impose their ways on those among whom they work. And when missionaries see both their faith/culture package *and* themselves as superior, they
may assume that those among whom they work should accommodate their
way of life to the missionaries' cultural norms.

Identifying the pastor as a professional within the corporate cultural
climate that currently pervades many mainline denominations encourages
some clergy to adopt similarly abusive approaches to ministry in small
churches located in rural areas.[2] Many pastors and denominational leaders
do seem frustrated by the issues that small, rural churches represent. According to popular measures, most small, rural congregations are not adequate. They are not financially self-sufficient. Even from the perspective of
their own leaders, most cannot provide an "adequate" salary for their
pastor (Walrath and Walrath, 1989). Often they struggle to maintain buildings that are old and inefficient. They cannot support a "full" program.
Leaders in small congregations are chronically overworked and seem inad-
equately trained for many of the responsibilities they assume. Small congregations have too few members to utilize most available stewardship
materials and education curricula. Many small congregations provide only
minimal financial support to their denomination. Most small churches are
not growing in numbers. In fact, the close interpersonal relationships
among the members seem to impede growth.

What is a pastor to do in such a congregation—especially when he or
she discovers that many of the implied "inadequacies" are not perceived as
such by members of congregations? In fact, members seem to assume:

—that the church will always need to make do economically;
—that pastors who really care for them will also willingly make do;
—that lay leaders are respected more for their willingness to serve than
   for their expertise;
—that current members are more valued than new members;
—that church members who resist giving money to support denominational work will give surprisingly large amounts of time, energy, and
   money to local mission work in which they are directly involved
   (Dudley, 1977; 1978; Ray, 1982; Smith, 1955; Walrath, 1979;
   Walrath and Walrath, 1988; 1989; Wicker, 1979).

Given the contrast between these attitudes and dynamics so common
among rural, small churches and both the organizational/programmatic

model of church and the professional model of ministry, it is not difficult to understand why pastors acculturated into the latter models are frustrated when they are called to minister with rural, small churches. Moreover, insofar as they shape their ministry according to the popular models, their frustration is likely to increase, for two reasons. (1) They are cast in a role similar to that of culturally insensitive missionaries. They appear to advocate ways of living and being the church that are neither appropriate nor possible in the judgment of many members of rural, small churches. (2) Some members of these churches stand ready to resist leaders "from away." Rural residents have increasingly discovered that they are a cultural minority and have learned to protect themselves against those who would impose unwelcome changes on them.

## The View from the Hinterlands

For nearly one hundred years residents of rural areas have seen their social and economic power wane (Fitchen, 1981). The roots of these losses are structural as well as economic. William J. Goodwin suggests that those who live at the edges and bottom of society have been more and more affected during recent decades by what he calls "scale-up" (Goodwin, n.d.). He describes a fundamental relocation of power, resources, and authority. Much of what was formerly decided, planned, and controlled locally is now decided, planned, and controlled at higher levels. Regional and national agencies of government now dominate local social services; large corporations dominate the workplace; large real estate groups control local development; even church program is now largely planned and implemented from regional and national levels.

Rural people generally have experienced loss in this widespread restructuring and redistribution of social and economic power. As their personal power pales and control passes to those "at the top," local interests often receive less consideration. For example, the needs and interests of local persons may exert little influence on the multinational corporation's decision to close a local facility, to clear-cut a forest, or to dump its hazardous waste.

The structural and functional changes associated with scale-up have also encouraged changes in self-image and sense of responsibility, on the part of both those at the top and those at the bottom of various systems and organizations. For example, with the growth of complex social agencies, local citizens concerned about adequate social services tend to view themselves less as individuals personally capable of or responsible for making a difference, and more as those who are called upon to support agencies that meet social needs on their behalf. The local citizen has little or no *direct* contact with those in need.

Many local church members have experienced a similar shift in roles. Denominations now assume collector and connector roles similar to social agencies, collecting resources from local congregations and dispensing those resources through agents (e.g., missionaries and other employed church workers and staff) or agencies (e.g., boards that make grants to support mission work or other worthwhile causes) that act in behalf of local church members. Individual church members now see themselves less as doers and more as supporters or sometimes, negatively, simply as those who are taxed.

Scale-up runs counter to many values and lifeways long characteristic of rural culture. Rural people characteristically resist standardization. They are accustomed to and prefer dealing with the problems and issues of life in their own way through direct action (Smith, 1955: chs. 1, 2). And, given the smaller scale and relative lack of complexity that is still typical of life in many rural areas, the traditional ways of direct action still seem functional to many rural people. In fact, in the judgment of some who live in these areas, the traditional, simpler, direct approaches work better than the changes ("development") urban outsiders would seek to impose (Berry, 1987; Sims, 1988).

Our research among pastors in small churches indicates that few pastors or denominational leaders appreciate the rural-culture perspectives I have just described. Most lay leaders affirm these perspectives—even persons who like me have moved from urban to rural locations later in life (Walrath and Walrath, 1988). Why the difference in viewpoints?

When outsiders to a culture feel superior to those within that culture, they are less likely to listen and learn from members of that culture. In a provocative book entitled *Rural Development: Putting the Last First*, Robert Chambers describes the tendency for highly schooled persons who move across cultures to be closed-minded, especially when they perceive the culture to which they go as inferior to the culture from which they come. During his study of First World efforts to improve agricultural production in Third World countries, Chambers often discovered such a closed mindset and way of proceeding among those at the center and top of technical organizations.

Western educational systems, especially those that prepare professionals, scientists, and technicians, assume a scale-up of knowledge. Those educated within these systems are led to believe that all *worthwhile* knowledge usually originates at the top or center of any organization or system and flows downward or outward. Those who internalize this perspective learn to see those located at the top or center of the organization that they represent as the sole sources of reliable insight. They always look toward the center or the top to gain insight. They do not consider those at the edges or the bottom as potential sources of insight or suggestions. A social position at the edge or the bottom indicates that someone is not likely to be a source of insight. On rare occasions, when professionals or technicians do listen to those who are at the bottom, they do so only in order to discover how to convince them to adopt whatever those in authority have decided is "good for them" (Chambers, 1983:75–102).

Chambers offers convincing evidence that these closed-minded technicians often advocate changes that are not practical or even possible for those among whom they work. They press "primitive" peoples to adopt practices that prove to be socially, economically, and psychologically unsound for them. But the technically educated persons' assumption that their culture is superior makes it difficult for them to gain insights from the others, insights that could reveal the flaws in what they advocate for them (Chambers, 1983:75–102).

The First World–Third World bias Chambers describes is remarkably similar to the urban-rural bias a Canadian analyst, R. Alex Sims, describes in his book *Land and Community: Crisis in Canada's Countryside* (1988). Sims suggests that urban biases now dominate North American culture. Rural areas are generally defined in subtle, negative terms, such as "the hinterland," "undeveloped," "lesser developed," "non-metropolitan." In fact, in 1976 the Library of Congress eliminated the word "rural" as a category from its classification system. Sims believes that rural areas are now viewed largely in terms of the ways they can be utilized or developed to benefit urban areas. He coins the phrase "urban imperialism" to describe the mind-set that sees the rural hinterland simply as a place to play in, develop, dump in, or extract from (1988).

Our interviews with pastors and lay leaders in rural congregations in connection with our 1986–1988 surveys indicate that pastors often bring a mind-set to rural ministry that resembles the First World–Third World and urban-rural biases described by Chambers and Sims. And my own interviews with denominational officials indicate that denominational systems reflect a similar bias.

Pastors we interviewed indicate that pastorates with rural, small churches are frequently assumed to be, and are even openly characterized within denominational circles as being, "on the bottom." Pastors who are appointed to rural parishes commonly believe they are seen by denominational officials, and often by their colleagues, as less able. Lay leaders of small churches affiliated with denominations that follow the call system of placement complain that their churches often seem able to attract only less experienced or less able ministers, perhaps because they are not able to pay sufficient salaries, or because so many pastors seem unwilling to live and serve small churches in rural areas (Walrath and Walrath, 1988; 1989).

Moreover, a perusal of available resources and suggested strategies for ministry with small churches reveals that such material rarely reflects the cultural characteristics of rural, small congregations. Educational materials usually assume a pool of Sunday school students large enough to form graded classes, or a pool of educationally qualified teachers able to devote considerable time to preparation. Stewardship materials assume that the needs of the church will be presented by visitors who have ample print or other visual resources available to them. Denominational mission literature points up mission as a "global" enterprise in which local persons are asked to participate by becoming informed and giving money.

Such material is largely unsuitable for use in rural, small congregations. Most of those who teach Sunday school in small congregations carry so many other leadership responsibilities in church and community life that they have little time to invest in preparation (Walrath, 1981:6). Members of small, rural congregations characteristically make their stewardship decisions together in a congregational gathering where they consider the needs of the church and its ministries (Oglesby, 1979; Pappas, 1989). They prefer to enter into mission through direct action (Kimber, 1987; Smith, 1955; Walrath, 1983:18–27).

## Some Suggestions

Pastors who would help small, rural congregations develop their potential need to enter, appreciate, and learn how to work within cultural ways that are native to those who compose these congregations. Doing so involves at least two steps. (1) The pastor must stay long enough in a parish to learn local ways and earn the trust of local people. (2) The pastor must be ready to exchange models of ministry and church shaped by the lifeways and culture out of which he or she comes for models that reflect the life-ways and culture within which he or she now ministers.

1. Most of the rural pastors described as "effective" by lay leaders we interviewed have served small congregations, and usually the same small congregation(s), for many years—often a decade or more. From our inter-views it appears that the most effective rural pastors do so well, in part, because they have served long enough in a rural parish to move beyond their urban biases to understand and embrace the lifeways of the people with whom they serve.

Genuine appreciation of the lifeways of those who live in a culture does seem indispensable for those who wish to become respected leaders in that culture. Before a pastor can be trusted to identify changes or developments that are appropriate and possible for those who compose the churches in a culture, he or she must appreciate them. And members of rural, small churches are more likely to trust the judgment of pastors who they feel have been with them long enough to understand and appreciate them. Both understanding and trust usually require many years to establish—espe-cially in instances where the pastor has no previous experience with rural culture or small churches. Pastors sensitive to the costs that change repre-sents to rural people are willing to remain with small churches long enough to help church members integrate the changes they introduce. Rural peo-ple are rightfully cautious: a powerful and culturally insensitive pastor may leave behind changes that do a great deal of damage.

2. Professional or managerial models of ministry and the related organi-zational/programmatic model of the church are generally inappropriate for rural pastors and for rural, small churches. A pastor who identifies herself or himself as a professional will have few peers in most rural, small congregations. A professional identity creates respect in an urban culture where professionals abound, but in a rural culture where professionals are rare, a professional identity creates distance from most people. If a rural pastor establishes a "professional" identity, a majority of his or her neigh-bors are put off. They see that pastor as someone beyond them, whose person and knowledge are not accessible to them.

A managerial identity is also usually not helpful. "Manager" is an orga-nizational or corporate identity. As I have already noted, most organiza-tions and corporate systems place rural people and institutions at the bottom or on the fringe. Rural people typically experience big government, corporations, and institutions generally as insensitive and inconsiderate of their needs and circumstances. A pastor who functions like a manager engages these feelings; such a pastor's concern for organizational effectiveness feels cold and calculating (Walrath, 1979:33–36).

Several years ago a middle-aged student who gave up farming to attend Bangor Seminary and prepare for ministry with rural congregations articulated a model of ministry that I have found rural people can affirm and rural pastors can employ as a model to guide them into effective ministry among rural people. After some experience as a student pastor in small congregations he suggested that a rural pastor in a small church is more like a dairy farmer than a professional or a manager. His own words describe why:

> When I would go to the barn on a winter morning, I never knew what I would find. A cow might be down [sick]; or the power out; or a water line frozen. I had to be ready to deal with anything, to fix whatever needed fixing.
>
> I never had enough time to do things right. I was always short of money; I never seemed to catch up with my bills. I was happy when I could just keep things going.
>
> But I loved that work and that life. While I never seemed to get ahead, I felt that what I did mattered.
>
> That's what ministry in a small church is like. You keep it going. You don't seem to accomplish much beyond helping others keep going. If you look carefully, sometimes you can see how much the church matters—how it helps people make it. Ministry is like going to the barn every day. You don't get ahead; but you know it matters.

Holding up such a model of ministry developed from within, rather than imposed upon, rural culture is helpful to rural pastors for two reasons: the way the model encourages them to see themselves as pastors, and what the model implies they will be able to accomplish.

Managerial and professional models of ministry encourage pastors to measure their performance against norms like growth and achievement. The dairy farmer model by contrast encourages pastors to evaluate their ministry in terms of the quality of their caregiving and their ability to make do with the resources available to them. The core values in this model are not urban values like organizational growth and development, but rural values like persistence and caring. This model also encourages pastors to think of ministry as a long-term investment, to recognize that returns in a rural ministry are likely to come only after many years of nurturing. Speed, achievement, advancement, and mobility are not appropriate cultural norms for rural ministers.

Innovation, however, is—especially innovation within the resources available. One of my farmer friends in Maine told me that he has persisted largely because he did not take the advice of outsiders, including "experts" from the U.S. Department of Agriculture. Three decades ago they advised him to concentrate on one kind of farming, to increase the size of his operation dramatically, and to borrow the money he needed to do so. He rejected the advice both because he believed it to be economically unsound and because he felt the changes they proposed would destroy the way of life associated with the family farm he values.

He proceeded in directions opposite from those the "experts" suggested. He kept his operation small and diversified. He limited his milking herd to twenty cows. He put the acreage not required to raise feed for his own herd into hay, which he sells. He and his wife purchased and planted many thousands of tree seedlings. And he borrowed very little money.

Neighboring farmers who specialized and enlarged their operations, borrowing large amounts of money to do so, are now struggling to survive (and some have been forced out of business by their losses), while my friend is quite comfortable. He currently milks about a dozen cows. He sells several thousand bales of hay each year. During the winter he cuts and hauls pulpwood from trees that have matured, using his farm tractor to drag out the wood, and the same truck he uses to haul hay in the summer he uses to haul logs to the pulp mill. The small, manageable scale of his operation, and his lack of dependence on any one product, protect him. In a single year the price has never been down on all three of the products he produces. At age sixty he has no debt. One day as we talked about his affection for his way of life he remarked, "I know you may find it hard to believe, but even after nearly forty years I still look forward to going to the barn to milk every morning."

Changes that are appropriate and possible enhance rather than destroy the institutions and practices that nurture a culture's way of life. In my consulting with rural congregations and during my ten years as a member of one of the small congregations affiliated with Mission-at-the-Eastward in Maine, I have seen sensitive and well-acculturated pastors introduce developments that vitalized the nurture and ministry of rural congregations. Though the twelve congregations that compose the mission are as small as they were a decade ago, they have become as faithful and effective in their life and ministries as any large, urban church I have ever seen. Through a housing ministry, for example, they reach out to rehabilitate more than a dozen houses each year. They were instrumental in beginning a computer components manufacturing firm five years ago to provide employment for displaced shoe industry workers. For twenty years they have engaged in a gardening ministry that helps the rural poor to learn to grow and process their own food. Recently they brought together a coalition of church, anti-poverty, state, and federal agencies to leverage a $1 million loan to purchase and rehabilitate the worst block of housing in Farmington, Maine—and sell it back to the residents (Kimber, 1987). Such ministries could not have been established without the leadership of our pastors. Nor is it happenstance that pastors able to facilitate these outstanding developments characteristically serve for many years. The current pastor who coordinates the work of the twelve churches has served the same three small churches for fifteen years. His two predecessors served for thirty-four years and twenty years.

Critics could point out that our congregations do not measure up to accepted organizational/programmatic norms for churches. They do not have a "full" program. While worship is vital and healthy, the Sunday schools are small. Only one of the congregations (which happens to be located in an area becoming suburban) has grown in size during the past decade. Giving increases each year in our parish of small churches, but despite the increases, we still struggle to pay our bills. Like the dairy farmer become pastor, we don't really expect to get ahead. Few people or churches do where we live. But we believe that what we do matters.

Pastors can survive and thrive in a rural ministry when that ministry is suitable for them, and when they plan to stay long enough to become culturally integrated. Of course, pastors (and spouses) who *require* the stimulation of urban culture usually do not do well in a rural ministry. In our research (Walrath and Walrath, 1988; 1989), pastors indicated that they move from rural parishes either because they dislike the isolation, the location is too remote from cultural activities and adequate medical services, educational opportunities are poor, they miss the stimulation of colleagues, or their salaries are not adequate.

But a pastor who wants to survive and thrive in rural ministry, and who *plans* to do so, likely will. One who plans to stay will invest deeply in forming friendships and establishing solid patterns of ministry. The economic rewards given to rural pastors are not so great as those given to pastors of larger, urban churches, but rural pastors who invest in their churches often find their churches investing in them. Likely the pastor's spouse (if she or he has one) will have to work to help support the household. A pastor who feels called to remain in a rural ministry may discover that she or he needs to emulate my farmer friend and develop several sources of income. My wife and I have done so. We derive some of our income from teaching, some from consulting, and some from writing. Denominational rules that make it difficult for pastors to accept other employment, and at the same time set minimum salaries that churches must pay to engage a pastor, are out of step with both rural culture and rural economics. Many rural families have developed innovative lifeways and happily work hard at a variety of jobs to be able to continue to live where they live. So can pastors and their families. And such pastors are likely to do well and remain in rural ministry.

I have not meant to give the impression in this chapter that pastors who enter a ministry with rural, small churches should accept the ways of rural culture and these churches uncritically. A pastor is never fully of the world he or she serves. A pastor always stands between as much as within: between the call of God and the calls of the congregation, and between the calls of the congregation and the calls of the larger church. But I do mean to imply that pastors who cannot stand within are likely to become imposing, and that such an imposition undermines their capacity to minister.

## NOTES

1. Material in this chapter is based primarily on data gathered during 1986, 1987, and 1988 from samples of pastors and lay leaders of small congregations in northern New England and northeastern New York. In all we gathered extensive data from seventy-eight pastors and forty-three lay leaders. In addition we conducted individual interviews with half the pastors and all the lay persons in our sample. The thoughts in the chapter also benefit from the observations of participants in a consultation on "Local Churches and Local Cultures" held at Bangor Theological Seminary in 1988. All of this research was supported by grants from the Lilly Endowment. Earlier versions of some of the material in this chapter appeared in *The Open Door*, Summer 1988 and Spring 1989.

2. For purposes of this discussion, small churches may be defined as congregations with not more than two hundred members. Rural areas are not restricted only to those with economies dependent on agriculture; they include economies based on other earth-related activities like mining and lumbering, sea-related economies, as well as more recently developed recreation and retirement communities.

## WORKS CITED

Berry, Wendell
    1987        *Home Economics*. Berkeley, Calif.: North Point Press.

Callahan, Kennon L.
    1983        *Twelve Keys to an Effective Church: Strategic Planning for Mission.* San Francisco: Harper & Row.

Chambers, Robert
    1983        *Rural Development: Putting the Last First.* New York: Longman.

Fitchen, Janet
    1981        *Poverty in Rural America—A Case Study.* Boulder, Colo.: Westview Press.

Goodwin, William J.
    n.d.        "Approaching Rural Ministry: A City Boy Plows Through Some Introductory Readings on Town and Country America." Washington, D.C.: Glenmary Research Center.

Hough, Joseph, and John Cobb
    1985        *Christian Identity and Theological Education.* Chico, Calif.: Scholars Press.

Hutchinson, William R.
    1987        *Errand to the World: American Protestant Thought and Foreign Missions.* Chicago: University of Chicago Press.

Kimber, Robert
    1987        "Man with a Mission." *DownEast* 34/5(December).

Merton, Robert K.
    1968        *Social Theory and Social Structure.* New York: Free Press.

Morton, T. Ralph
    1951        *The Household of Faith: An Essay on the Changing Pattern of the Church's Life.* Glasgow: Iona Community.
    1956        *The Twelve Together.* Glasgow: Iona Community.

O'Connor, Elizabeth
    1963        *Call to Commitment: The Story of the Church of the Saviour, Washington, D.C.* New York: Harper & Row.

Oglesby, Frank
    1979        "The Every Member Uncanvass: A Stewardship Kit for Small Congregations." Luling, Tex.: Resource Center for Small Churches.

Pappas, Anthony J.
    1989        *Keeping the Small Church Afloat: Ministry, Motivation and Stewardship.* Valley Forge, Pa.: Judson Press.

Peters, Thomas J., and Robert H. Waterman, Jr.
    1984        *In Search of Excellence: Lessons from America's Best-run Companies.* New York: Warner Books.

Ray, David R.
    1982        *Small Churches Are the Right Size.* New York: Pilgrim Press.

Roof, Wade Clark
1978        *Community and Commitment: Religious Plausibility in a Liberal Protestant Church.* New York: Elsevier/North-Holland.

Roof, Wade Clark, and William McKinney
1987        *American Mainline Religion: Its Changing Shape and Future.* New Brunswick, N.J.: Rutgers University Press.

Schutz, Roger
1962        *Living Today for God.* Baltimore: Helicon Press.

Sims, R. Alex
1988        *Land and Community: Crisis in Canada's Countryside.* Guelph, Ont.: University of Guelph.

Smith, Rockwell C.
1955        *The Church in Our Town.* Nashville: Abingdon Press.

Wagner, C. Peter
1984        *Your Church Can Grow.* Ventura, Calif.: Regal Books.

Walrath, Douglas Alan
1979        *Leading Churches Through Change.* Nashville: Abingdon Press.
1981        "Finding Options for Ministry in Small Churches." New York: National Council of Churches.
1983        *New Possibilities for Small Churches.* New York: Pilgrim Press.
1988        *Options: How to Develop and Share Christian Faith Today.* New York: Pilgrim Press.

Walrath, Sherry, and Douglas Alan Walrath
1988        "Supporting Small Congregations and Their Pastors: Some Issues and Possibilities." *The Open Door* (Summer).
1989        "What Helps Pastors to Be Effective in Small Churches." *The Open Door* (Spring).

Wicker, Allan W.
1979        *An Introduction to Ecological Psychology.* Monterey, Calif.: Brooks/Cole Publishing Co.

# NINE

# Congregations' Educational Strategy
## C. ELLIS NELSON

The congregation is at the center of Christians' spiritual life. It is the place where Christians worship, celebrate the sacraments, study the Bible, organize themselves for service, and help each other as life unfolds with its joys, sorrows, and moments when critical decisions must be made. Because the congregation is central, it is also the unit of the larger church most directly concerned about interpreting and communicating the faith to the rising generation.

This essay describes the educational strategy used by congregations of "mainstream" denominations, traces the historical conditions that led these denominations to rely on the Sunday school as their educational agency, reviews optional strategies, and concludes with the proposal that the congregation itself be the agency of education. Congregations of other denominations that have depended on a school model of education may find the proposed congregational model helpful as they evaluate their strategy.

## The Strategy Issue

Congregational strategy should be distinguished from denominational strategy. Mainstream denominations have—over a period of time—developed a variety of educational institutions and programs that, taken together, represent their educational strategy. Denominations have founded seminaries to educate their ministers, colleges to influence lay leaders for church and society, training institutes for missionaries and lay leaders, summer conference centers for teenagers, and more recently, television programs for the home or for use in church school classes. Denominational strategy is essential for the well-being of the church at large but is not the subject of this chapter. The purpose of this chapter is to suggest how congregations of mainstream denominations can more effectively educate themselves, their children, and new members in the Christian faith.

A congregation's strategy is the deliberate means by which it plans to communicate and interpret the Christian faith. There are many informal occasions in which church members educate and influence each other, such as through conversations during church night suppers or in committee meetings; but this essay is primarily about *planned* educational programs.

If we were to ask average members of a mainstream Protestant congregation to describe their educational program, the answer would probably be as follows: "We have a Sunday school for children, a youth class or group, and some adult Bible classes." If the congregation had a special interest in education, the respondent might add, "and we have a vacation Bible school and send some of our young people to summer camp."

If we were to continue our probe and ask the average church member whether this strategy for Christian education was adequate for the present situation, the answer would be no. They would say there is not enough time in the typical Sunday school class to do very much; attendance at Sunday school is irregular; and many teachers are poorly prepared for their work. Moreover, because of the time restraints there is very little opportunity for students to relate their personal life situation to the biblical or theological material under consideration. The resulting education is a smattering of knowledge of Christianity and a partial understanding of what beliefs and practices are required of church members.

Why, then, do congregations continue this school strategy? One reason is that much good comes out of the Sunday school, youth groups, and Bible classes. This may be due to the personal interest the teachers take in the children or the support some of the members get from their peers. Inertia also contributes to the continuation of the school strategy, for congregations tend to do what they have been doing. Lay people who staff the educational program have little time for church involvement other than the traditional Sunday school program. Also, there is a lack of historical knowledge about how the Sunday school became the congregation's educational strategy. If we had a better understanding of our history, we would be able to see why the Sunday school cannot carry the educational burdens we lay on it today.

## Why the Sunday School Strategy?

Robert W. Lynn has given special attention to issues related to educational strategy. Lynn's first written presentation of the history of Protestant educational strategy was his doctoral dissertation, a portion of which was expanded and published as *Protestant Strategies in Education* (Lynn, 1964a). Later he wrote a widely read history of the Sunday school entitled *The Big Little School* (Lynn and Wright, 1971). In these publications Lynn has shown how Protestants responded to changing social conditions so that, by the early 1960s, when the Supreme Court ruled that school prayer was illegal and that teaching of religion could only be done "objectively," there was not much left except the Sunday school and other church-sponsored classes. The gradual dependence on the Sunday school as the Protestant strategy of education is a long and complex story. The following is a shortened and simplified version of the important facts (Nelson, 1989, chapter 10).

*The Nineteenth Century*

The United States in the nineteenth century was concerned about building a nation with a democratic form of government of a kind for which there was no historical precedent and out of a continent not yet fully explored. At the beginning of the century there were twenty-two states, all east of the Mississippi River. At the end of the century there were fifty states or territories, including Hawaii and Alaska. At the beginning of the century the population was 5,306,486. At the end of the century the population was 76,212,168 of which about 25 percent were immigrants, mostly from Western European countries.

At the beginning of the nineteenth century there was no public school system; at the end of it free education through high school was available almost everywhere in the nation. Although New York State formed the first school system in 1812, Massachusetts is considered the leader in the state-supported common school movement. This was due to the leadership of Horace Mann, who became the first executive secretary of the State Board of Education in 1837. Through his leadership and the *Common School Journal,* which he edited, the cause of tax-supported public education was advanced throughout the nation. Connecticut followed Massachusetts, establishing a board of education in 1848 and appointing Henry Barnard its secretary. Later Barnard organized the Rhode Island school system, founded the *American Journal of Education* (1855), and became the first United States Commissioner of Education (1867).

Although Horace Mann and Henry Barnard were personally religious, they believed the state-supported schools should not teach religion. This was due in part to the separation of church and state by the Bill of Rights (1791) and in part to the rivalry of denominations as they sought to have their particular doctrines taught in public schools. Mann and Barnard never tired of telling church leaders that they had the Sunday school in which they could teach their doctrines. As a result, religion was slowly squeezed out of the public schools. Two American historians, James Hastings Nichols and Sydney Mead, looking back on this separation of religion from education, judged it to be a decisive turning point in American culture; it compartmentalized religion into the church and it secularized public education (Kennedy, 1966:71–72).

The gradual separation of religion from public schools was apparent to church leaders. Roman Catholics, who were immigrating to the United States in large numbers before the Civil War, realized that they could not change the Protestant atmosphere of the public schools and could not prevent their secularization, so they established parochial schools. Some Lutheran denominations also founded day schools. Presbyterians, realizing that the public schools were being secularized, started to found elementary schools about 1847, but the disruption of the Civil War caused them to abandon the effort about 1870.

Mainstream Protestant denominations in the middle of the nineteenth century found themselves being excluded from public schools and religion itself becoming less important to public schools. This would have been an intolerable situation if the Sunday school movement had not taken root in American soil. The Sunday school, as it originated in England in 1780, was for poor children who did not attend day schools. Such a purpose did not fit the American situation, as the public school system was growing rapidly in the first half of the nineteenth century. However, the Sunday school as a parachurch movement for teaching religion solved the problem of how to transmit religion to the next generation, for congregations could easily start a Sunday school.

This practical solution for religious instruction fitted the religious situation of that era. The nineteenth century was dominated by the Second Great Awakening, a form of evangelistic theism that continues in our time as evangelical Christianity. This Protestant passion for conversion to Christianity and for the establishment of a "righteous empire" in this new land was especially strong until the Civil War (Marty, 1970). Revivals emerged in New England, Virginia, Kentucky, and on the western frontier. Evangelistic Christianity also dominated many colleges. For example, Timothy Dwight, president of Yale College, preached a series of sermons in 1802 and one-third of the student body responded by making a profession of faith. Most of the colleges founded prior to the Civil War were founded by Protestant denominations. From these colleges came the leaders of church and society who through their vocations inculcated the enthusiasm and beliefs of evangelical Christianity. In 1855 it was estimated that ten thousand of the forty thousand graduates of American colleges had become ministers. The ministry had great appeal for young men, as Donald Tewksbury observed, because "the church in that day was an active force in society and under the leadership of able men it took a prominent part in the social, political, and intellectual interests of the day" (Tewksbury, 1932:69).

The religious mood of the first half of the nineteenth century was well expressed by Horace Bushnell in an essay entitled "Barbarism the First Danger" (1847):

> The wilderness shall bud and blossom as the rose before us; and we will not cease, till a Christian nation throws up its temples of worship on every hill and plain; till knowledge, virtue and religion, blending their dignity and their healthful power, have filled our great country with a manly and happy race of people, and the bands of a complete Christian commonwealth are seen to span the continent (Handy, 1971:24).

The Sunday school fitted this evangelistic enthusiasm to create a Christian nation out of the wilderness. It had two powerful organizations promoting its expansion and welfare. One was the American Sunday School Union, founded in 1824. This Sunday school union was led primarily by lay people with a strong evangelistic interest. In 1830 the union voted to establish within two years "a Sunday School in every destitute place where it is practicable, throughout the valley of the Mississippi." The territory they had in mind covered two-thirds of the land mass of the nation (Lynn and Wright, 1971:41).

The Sunday school was a movement to evangelize people into a general Protestant theology. A Sunday school could be started by lay people, so there were no ecclesiastical problems related to ordination or sacraments. This worked well on the frontier. In fact, Henry Barnard observed that on the western frontier the Sunday school was often "the precursor and pioneer both of the district school and of the church" (Kennedy, 1966:21).

The second promotional agency was the denomination. Seeing the need to provide religious instruction for children, the denominations began to establish departments to promote the Sunday school and to publish curriculum materials. By 1872 these efforts resulted in the International Uniform Lessons, a development that stabilized the Sunday school movement and gave it considerable educational status in the churches.

The Sunday school as a nineteenth-century strategy for evangelizing children and youth and for providing religious instruction as the public schools became secular was a success. It achieved these goals because it was a supplement to other means of communicating the Christian faith. First, the ethos of the culture, especially up to the Civil War, was Christian. Revival meetings in all areas of the country over a long period of time, the "circuit rider" system of the Methodist Church for providing religious services on the frontier, and the formation of new denominations in Kentucky and Tennessee based on "religious experience" all stem from the same underlying theology. Although the public schools were dissociating themselves from the churches, McGuffey's *Readers* were used by four out of five children from 1836 to 1900. These readers, written from the perspective of Calvinist theology, contained Bible lessons and prayers, and more than half of the lessons were devoted to moral education (Westerhoff, 1978:15). So a religious interpretation of life was communicated to children as they learned to read. Alexis de Tocqueville, in his visit to the United States in the 1830s, summed it up in these words: "There is no country in the world where the Christian religion retains a greater influence over the souls of men than in America" (Hudson, 1965:130).

Second, the Protestant churches had great influence in society. This was due in part to the rapid expansion of congregations. Winthrop Hudson estimates that one out of fifteen persons in 1800 were church members. By 1835 one out of eight were church members. However, church membership in those days was rather strict, so church attendance was higher than membership. By 1830 about three times as many people attended church as were members. The United States census for 1860 shows a total of 54,745 churches with a seating capacity of about nineteen million people in a nation of about thirty-one million (Hudson, 1965:129–135).

Third, the home was an agency for inculcating Christian beliefs and morals. America was primarily a rural society even toward the end of the century. Victorian ideas controlled family life during this period. The father was the head of the family, the mother looked after the physical and developmental needs of the children. Children helped out with household chores, which had immediate relevance to their lives, such as cooking, washing clothes, or bringing in firewood. Rural families were somewhat isolated, so except for school or church the children were under the influence of their parents most of the time.

### The Twentieth Century

At the beginning of the twentieth century the Sunday school was well established as the congregational strategy for education. The public schools were secular, although remnants of religious influence were carried over in opening prayers, Bible readings, and Christmas celebrations. Congregations, trying to shore up their educational efforts, began to use the summertime for Bible schools, camps, and conferences. Church leaders, realizing that the separation of church from state in public schools was complete, set about to find ways to coordinate their concerns. Two plans emerged.

One plan was for the church to have a period during the public school schedule when children could attend classes in religion on a voluntary basis. The "released time" plan as devised in Gary, Indiana, in 1914 became the pattern. The "released time" plan spread rapidly, but it was declared unconstitutional by the Supreme Court in 1948. The Supreme Court ruled in 1952 that teaching religion during school hours was constitutional if it took place off school property, but the obstacles to such a plan are so great that it has not become a viable option for the churches.

Another plan was for church weekday schools to share time with the public school. In this "shared time" plan, church weekday schools would teach religion and other "value-oriented" subjects, and the public schools would teach the rest of the curriculum (Lynn, 1966:329–340). An early version of this plan was proposed by Walter S. Athearn in 1917 for the town of Walden, Massachusetts.

Athearn made a critical analysis of all organizations, agencies, and institutions offering religious education and a summary of over six hundred articles and books concerning the problems involved in having a nationwide religious education program related to public schools. He was motivated by the need of a democracy to have educated citizens with religious and moral training. He knew that Bible reading and prayer in public schools were inadequate. He judged the Sunday school in these words: "Utilize it and standardize it as you may, the Sunday session of the church school will not furnish an adequate religious education for our people" (Athearn, 1917:113).

Athearn's plan did not succeed and more recent versions have not been acceptable. But Athearn is to be commended for his realistic appraisal both of the need for the religious and moral education of all children and of the inability of the churches to serve the nation with their Sunday school. The remnants of religion in public schools continued well into the twentieth century, but the Supreme Court in 1962 ruled prayer in public school was unconstitutional. In 1963, in the *School District of Abington Township v. Schempp* case, the Supreme Court ruled a devotional reading of the Bible unconstitutional. Justice Tom Clark in the majority opinion ruled that public schools could teach religion only "when presented objectively as part of the secular program of education." This principle gave the final definition of public schools as secular institutions.

## The Strategy Issue Today

As indicated above, the Sunday school as the principal agency of instruction became the church's strategy in the early part of the nineteenth century. It was a success at that time because it fitted into a social situation characterized by a Protestant ethos, it was a time when churches had great influence over individuals and communities, ministers were among the best educated leaders, and home was the place where Christian character was formed. As the state schools became secularized and as the nation became industrialized and urbanized, church leaders in the twentieth century saw the inadequacies of the Sunday school as a weekly instructional period. Many efforts have been made since the early 1900s to supplement or enhance the effectiveness of the Sunday school or to create a dual system of instruction by some kind of alliance with public schools. In reviewing these efforts to find a usable strategy, Lynn labels them "a history of failure" (Lynn, 1964a:49).

Since the matter of educational strategy has been before Protestants since the early 1800s, the three options are well known.

First, Protestants can continue their present strategy and attempt to improve all its parts. This would mean trying to make congregational life more meaningful, home experience more stable and more informed by the faith and morals of the church, and Sunday school and the age-group organizations more significant. This is not a bad scenario, yet mainstream Protestants have been using these efforts to revitalize the existing agencies of education without much success. There are limitations to this school-centered design because our social situation has changed.

The second option is for Protestants to develop parochial schools. The idea of Christians having their own day schools reasserts itself when existing schools are of poor quality, are dominated by other religions, or are too secular, or when the Christian group has particular doctrines it is determined to teach. Some Lutheran groups, the Christian Reformed Church, and some sect groups have established and maintained day schools for a long time. Since the 1960s conservative and fundamental churches have increasingly established day schools because they believed the public school curriculum was too secular or the moral conditions within the student body were too permissive. Mainstream Protestants, however, do not have the money or motivation to establish a system of parochial schools; they will not do so unless social conditions become much worse.

The third option is for mainstream Protestants to develop the congregation as a community of believers seeking God's will for their lives and communicating their faith and practice to children and nonbelievers through the congregation's natural channels of influence. This option requires adults to take responsibility for the interpretation and communication of the faith. In practical terms this means that the congregation must become conscious of itself as a community in which teaching and learning are going on incessantly and must organize itself to be the center for interpreting the faith. There will be classes for instruction but not as an adjunct to the life of the congregation—as most Sunday school classes now function.

## Congregation as Agent of Education

The third option is the one that fits our situation today. We are living in a secular society, the values of which are communicated to families through television, peer groups, public schools, and government programs. Individuals—especially children—are almost powerless against the dominant culture unless they belong to a group that has different values and goals.

Congregations are different from other social institutions. Although congregations have property, a form of government, legal status, and a history as do other institutions, they are different because of their beliefs. The beliefs form a community of like-minded people who share like-minded concerns. The idea of congregation comes from the Old Testament. However, as a voluntary association of believers engaged in study and worship in order to be right with God, it is most clearly described in the New Testament (Birch, 1988:20–42).

The communal aspect of the congregation is profoundly educational. When people share the meaning of life and death with friends and participate in each other's decisions, a strong bonding takes place. This bonding or "fellowship of kindred minds" creates an openness to congregational experiences. Worship, for example, with its prayers, music, scripture, sermon, and sacraments, stimulates, instructs, and guides the minds of believers. The content of worship—particularly the sermon—and informal conversations of members define an approved style of life. The way the congregation conducts its affairs also has educational potential. Members learn how the values of religion are translated into practical policies as congregations make decisions regarding budgets, show concern for human conditions in the community, or allow the use of buildings and equipment by outside groups.

The best illustration of how the natural processes of the community educate is to observe how they work in a sect. For example, congregations of the Seventh-day Adventist Church conduct their worship on Saturday. They believe in a personal, visible return of Jesus Christ to reign for a thousand years "at a time unknown but close at hand." These and other beliefs—such as keeping one's body free of alcohol, tobacco, and other harmful substances so it will be a fit place for the Spirit of God—are taught in their schools and are modeled in the lives of adult members. The communal life of such congregations will teach these beliefs in everything they do, and the beliefs will be modeled and explained by parents to their children. Sect congregations communicate their beliefs so effectively that they hardly need a Sunday school except to provide peer fellowship for children and youth.

Congregations of mainstream denominations are not and will not become sects. They are, however, different to some extent from the surrounding culture. The problem is how to help such congregations become more like the faith they profess so their communal aspect will become more effective in communicating the meaning of faith to themselves and to their children.

*How the Strategy Works*

The strategy for solving the problem is the same as the one used by Paul with the Corinthians (1 Cor. 14). Paul insisted that the leaders of the congregation engage in a sustained study of Christian beliefs in relation to events taking place in their lives in order to forge a Christian mentality. Not only the struggle to find the meaning of life but the meaning itself could be communicated to children by parents and to outsiders by adults as they went about their normal activities. In this small, intense community of believers, it was unnecessary to have a Sunday school for children or separate classes for adults. The congregation itself was the place where learning took place.

As previously indicated, this strategy works very well today for sect groups. Religious beliefs are so well ingrained in sect groups and in some congregations—both liberal and conservative—that members will, according to their beliefs, refuse to salute the American flag, refuse certain medical treatments, regularly give a high percentage of their income to the congregation, work long hours to protest or to protect legislation related to their beliefs, or in some other way live counter to cultural values.

Why does this strategy work? The answer in part is that congregations of sect groups or congregations that have a distinctive mission are often small and their members can share their life experiences in relation to their religious beliefs. Through this process their congregations become the primary group to which they turn for guidance and support as they try to live according to their beliefs. But some large congregations and even some religious movements such as the Quakers have also been able to maintain a distinctive way of life. The basic reason is the power of beliefs. A congregation is crucial in this regard because there the members can formulate their beliefs in relation to decisions they must make, test their beliefs in relation to events as they occur, and receive support from others with similar problems and commitments.

Will this strategy work with congregations of mainstream denominations? Recent studies are not very encouraging. Many congregations seem to live by a guiding principle or major interest that may not allow for openness to change (Roozen, McKinney, and Carroll, 1984:23–36; Dudley, 1988:89–114). For example, a congregation may be primarily concerned to provide religious support for civic values. Members, being active in business, professional, or educational matters, may expect the congregation to affirm the status quo. Another congregation may have a long history of representing a cross section of opinions about religion. Members expect the church to bridge or obscure differences of belief in order to promote fellowship or service to the community. Another congregation may emphasize its historical tradition, with little regard for current conditions. Can these congregations change the beliefs that underlie their interpretation of Christianity?

I think congregations can change their beliefs. Preaching, however, will seldom bring about change, for the sermon within the context of worship does not allow for an exchange of ideas. It will be necessary for ministers to engage adults who are at the center of the church's life with a systematic study of the Bible and theology over a long period of time. The educational setting must allow adults a chance to suggest the study agenda, time to respond to the teacher, and an opportunity to share their faith experiences.

*A Practical Proposal*

There are several ways ministers and a few key leaders could proceed to change the ethos of a congregation. One practical plan would be for the minister to develop a central study group (CSG). This center of energy, vision, and spiritual discipline is designed to shape the congregation's purpose and mission. I have worked out the details of this plan and applied it to different types and sizes of congregations in *How Faith Matures* (Nelson, 1989: ch. 11). The following is a very brief description of the proposal.

The CSG should consist of the ministers, officers, teachers, and interested adults. The purpose is to "build up" the congregation. It is not a conventional adult Sunday school class that aims at the education of individuals. The CSG must be led by the ministers, for they are the authorized and recognized leaders of the congregation. This does not mean the ministers do all the teaching, but it means they preside and take charge of discussions even if someone else teaches for a time. The CSG will require a major commitment of time and energy from the ministers, but it should not take more study time, because the sermons are expected to come from CSG discussions. The CSG will need a planning committee. This will be a small group selected by the ministers to manage the enterprise. One of their responsibilities is to help the minister select themes or topics to be explored in the CSG. Topics must be for the edification of the congregation. This requires judgment about the spiritual needs of the congregation. Topics must also be about something that requires decisions. This means the matter selected for study must have some connection with the lives of people in the congregation. With these criteria in mind, the planning committee may decide on a serious and sustained study of the Lord's Prayer, the Apostles' Creed, or a book of the Bible that is most appropriate to their situation.

Another task of the planning committee is to monitor the educational process. The CSG is an on-going group of the most interested and active people in the congregation. Changes in procedure may be needed from time to time. Members of the planning committee should talk informally with the people involved in this CSG in order that the time be used effectively. For example, ministers tend to think members understand the special meaning of commonly used words such as "grace," "kingdom of God," or "evil." Today, many middle-aged adults in our congregations have had very little Christian education and probably do not understand the special religious significance of the words being used in the church.

### Educational Process

The CSG should meet once a week for about an hour. Except for an opening prayer, the time should be devoted to study.

The study time is not a lecture with a few questions from the class. Rather, the group is expected to generate practical theology. This means that members must discuss issues. One way is to start with books of the Bible or theological statements and to set up ways for the people to respond out of their experience. Another way is to start with life situations and relate them to the Christian tradition. But either way there must be interaction between the minister/teacher and the group, because a major purpose is to create meaning for our times.

Probably the most difficult problem is how to deal with the preconceptions members bring to the CSG. Because members are only dimly aware of their assumptions, they may become defensive or aggressive when these assumptions are challenged. Success, for example, may be a problem. Many mainstream Protestants put a high value on competence and achievement. This value is not good or bad in itself, but it can be distorted. If adults think that success—as measured in terms of money or status—can be obtained by anyone who just works hard enough, then we have a serious problem. From a Christian point of view, success could be living a good life with low income and a simple job.

Other illustrations of presuppositions people bring to congregational life are some men's condescending attitudes toward women, the belief that all poor people are poor because they fail to take advantage of opportunities, the assumption that misfortune is punishment for misbehavior, or the notion that if people keep the moral laws they will be rewarded.

Bringing predispositions to the surface where their role in interpreting the Christian faith can be examined and evaluated is a complex procedure. Most adults are comfortable with their assumptions and do not want to acknowledge or change them. About the only practical way we can help church members become wiser about themselves is to encourage them to explain the basis on which they make decisions and to provide opportunities for them to do so. The CSG should be organized to allow for small group discussions. In small groups, members are freer to say why they hold the position they do and to relate their reasons to their life experiences. By this process the members begin to become more objective about themselves and more open to other views.

It is important to emphasize that this study group has no administrative duties and provides no governing functions for the congregation. By keeping the purpose of study clear, there should be no criticism that an elite group is being formed to run the church. Study of the kind described in this paper requires an examination of one's values, of how one's assumptions came to be, and of how they are used to interpret the Bible. Such an examination is difficult. It is time-consuming and somewhat threatening to one's settled lifestyle. Thus, the CSG is more a process of spiritual transformation than it is the acquisition of knowledge. Not every adult is ready or willing to participate in such a venture. That is why the minister should develop the group over a period of time.

The purpose of the CSG is to provide a center where ministers, officers, teachers, and interested adults can develop a practical theology for the congregation. From this center ministers will get substance for their sermons, concerns for their pastoral prayers, and an opportunity to influence congregational leaders. Officers will receive a sense of direction and a theological basis for making decisions for the congregation. Teachers will be inspired for their work and guided in biblical interpretation. Participants who are parents should experience a maturation of their faith so they will become better role models for their children.

## New Orientation

This proposal to consider the congregation, rather than the Sunday school, as the agency of education does not eliminate the Sunday school. Children need church-sponsored classes to learn the Christian tradition with their peers. In large churches youth and adult groups need classes for their special interests. What is different is an understanding that the classes only supplement what the congregation is doing as it interprets the gospel in worship and mission. The purpose is to help the congregation become a Christian community where members receive inspiration and guidance to orient their lives toward God and not toward the values of a secular society.

### WORKS CITED

Athearn, Walter S.
    1917          *Religious Education and American Democracy.* Boston: Pilgrim Press.

Birch, Bruce C.
    1988          "Memory in Congregational Life," in C. Ellis Nelson, ed., *Congregations: Their Power to Form and Transform.* Atlanta: John Knox Press.

Dudley, Carl S.
    1988        "Using Church Images for Commitment, Conflict, and Re-
                newal." In C. Ellis Nelson, ed., *Congregations: Their Power to
                Form and Transform.* Atlanta: John Knox Press.

Handy, Robert T.
    1971        *A Christian America.* New York: Oxford University Press.

Hudson, Winthrop S.
    1965        *Religion in America.* 2nd edition. New York: Charles
                Scribner's Sons.

Kennedy, William B.
    1966        *The Shaping of Protestant Education.* New York: Association
                Press.

Lynn, Robert W.
    1964a       *Protestant Strategies in Education.* New York: Association
                Press.
    1964b       "The Making of an American." In Roger L. Shinn, *The Search
                for Identity,* pp. 119–133. New York: Harper & Row.
    1966        "The Public Schools and the Study of Religion." In Marvin J.
                Taylor, ed., *An Introduction to Christian Education,* pp. 329–
                340. Nashville: Abingdon Press.
    1973        "Civil Catechetics in Mid-Victorian America: Some Notes
                About American Civil Religion, Past and Present." *Religious
                Education* (January-February): 5–28.
    1976        "A Historical Perspective on the Futures of American Reli-
                gious Education." In Marvin J. Taylor, ed., *Foundations for
                Christian Education in an Era of Change,* pp. 7–20. Nashville:
                Abingdon Press.

Lynn, Robert W., and Elliott Wright
    1971        *The Big Little School.* Nashville: Abingdon Press.

Marty, Martin E.
    1970        *Righteous Empire.* New York: Dial Press.

Nelson, C. Ellis
    1989        *How Faith Matures.* Louisville, Ky.: Westminster/John Knox
                Press.

Roozen, David A., William McKinney, and Jackson W. Carroll
    1984        *Varieties of Religious Presence.* New York: Pilgrim Press.

Tewksbury, Donald G.
    1932        *The Founding of American Colleges and Universities before the
                Civil War.* New York: Teachers College, Columbia University.

Westerhoff, John H.
    1978        *McGuffey and His Readers.* Nashville: Abingdon Press.

# TEN

# Community and Contentiousness: Lessons from the RENEW Program

## JAMES R. KELLY

Churches are by definition constantly in need of renewal. They are always bound to disappoint anyone who attaches an important part of herself or himself to their life. Since they promise so much even in simply human terms—the experience of community—churches themselves are a prime cause of disillusionment. Without ideals, there are no disappointments. What churches promise is so beyond human capacity that disappointment must be one of their chief characteristics. Ministers know this, seminarians suspect it, and members endure it. We seek renewal not only of our own spirit but of the church that nurtures and challenges us.

But how to renew and what constitutes renewal are not always easily answered. Efforts at renewal often bring about disagreements and contention. Religious traditions, and local congregations, need help to affirm community amid contention. Renewal and reconciliation must be sought together. A constant task of the church is to stimulate thinking about ways that religious traditions can find "structures of reconciliation" and in this way help ordinary men and women experience the religious bond as more primary than the immediate resolution of contentious issues. A communal focus for spiritual renewal and reconciliation was the chief aspiration of RENEW, an approach adopted by many thousands of Roman Catholic parishes. Lilly Endowment funding enabled me to study the RENEW program and to think about what we might learn from it.

## RENEW: Origins and Rationale

There has never been a more widespread program of explicit renewal than RENEW, which began in September 1977. A decade later one hundred twelve dioceses, including some in Ireland, Australia, Canada, and Belize, had RENEW programs. Since so many different dioceses from so

many different countries adopted the same program, there is good reason
to believe that the RENEW founders have hit upon a particularly persuasive definition of the situation of contemporary Catholicism. There might
be lessons here for other churches as well.

RENEW began in Newark, New Jersey, which is hardly the place
(across the river and southwest of Manhattan) one would predict as the
source of an innovative program that, just about one decade after its humble beginnings, had been adopted by over a hundred different dioceses in
almost a dozen different countries. My first contact with the RENEW
director, Msgr. Tom Kleissler, was richly suggestive. His initial description
went something like this: You can no longer expect your children to be
Roman Catholic with the same confidence that your parents had about
their children. All the old supports are gone. Modern culture to some
degree tolerates religion but it no longer supports religious belief. For
Catholicism to continue, parishes must themselves evangelize Catholics.
Since religion in contemporary society is "voluntary," parishes must become "intentional" communities. They must become warmer and friend-
lier, and they must find ways of fostering a more communal spirituality.

Anyone from any religious tradition might say something similar about
religion in contemporary secularist societies.

Msgr. Kleissler attributes the originating notion of RENEW, especially
its communal focus, to himself, a pastor, and to the Rev. Thomas Ivory,
who had directed religious education in the Archdiocese of Newark. During his studies in 1972 at the University of Louvain, Ivory learned of the
newly developed Rite of Christian Initiation (RCIA), where small groups of
lay parishioners are involved in the preparation of adult converts for baptism. The RCIA program taught that the already baptized *also* needed
conversion and that the reception of new members should be the occasion
for parish renewal. RCIA held that if a church presumes to receive converts, the receiving parish must also be converted. Converts become the
occasion not for congregational self-congratulation but for renewing the
sense of discipleship of the local church.

Kleissler himself had been involved in many of the lay "movements"
found in Catholicism during the previous two decades, such as the Christian Family Movement, Catholic Action, Young Christian Students, and
ecumenical living room dialogues. In all these movements, small groups
were prominent and they became the centerpiece of RENEW. Common to
these movements were the emphasis on lay involvement and the critique of
any clerical culture that led to lay passivity. RENEW teaches that everyone

in every parish should have a ministry. RENEW tries to create an environment where the Protestant ideal of the priesthood of all believers is actually practiced. Catholic lay people, for the most part, needed not only encouragement but structured help to realize this aspiration.

## The Proximate and Pragmatic Origin of RENEW

The experiences of Kleissler and Ivory in involving laity in small groups and mobilizing them for more active involvement provided a remote preparation for RENEW. The proximate catalyst was the decision in 1974 by the archbishop of Newark, Peter L. Gerety, that all parishes in the diocese should have parish councils. Kleissler in turn argued persuasively that it made little sense to erect by decree a new parish structure prompted by the Second Vatican Council if there was an underdeveloped consciousness of the council's teachings about the mission of the church and the role of the laity.

Preparation for the mandated parish councils was done by a newly created Office of Pastoral Renewal. Its first meetings were attended by twenty members. It is worth noting that this group met with no specific design and began with "brainstorming" discussions, an indication of the uncertainty of this period of Roman Catholic history. There was no hierarchically approved plan for parish renewal for this era of Roman Catholicism. The art of induction from shared experience would have to provide the methodology for renewal.

This inductive and "brainstorming" approach ensured a program that built on pastoral experience and aimed at inclusiveness. If a group is representative and the discussions are long enough, no interest is likely to be omitted. (Later we will see how RENEW with the aid of a bishops' committee sought to prevent inclusiveness from declining into formlessness.) Program decisions were based on what experience teaches. For example, Kleissler remarked that he had learned from years of parish experience that when he asked parishioners to do something "next week," they often refused; but when he asked if they might help "in the coming months," they did. Examples of a hands-on expertise learned only by active local involvement abound in RENEW.

RENEW began in September 1977 and the RENEW written material was developed and then altered as the program went along. Kleissler said that this constant feedback convinced them that the material should be largely scriptural, rather than doctrinal, and that the materials be kept simple. Shared religious experience became the point of RENEW, not formation in correct doctrine. Kleissler explained that "the point of RENEW was not so much coming to seek doctrinal answers as to grow spiritually through the exchange of spiritual experience." A major part of RENEW is the effort to make people feel Catholic without defining what being Catholic might mean in precise doctrinal terms. It should be noted that later a bishops' committee successfully recommended that more explicitly doctrinal matters be incorporated into RENEW material. But this too is something that others might wish to reflect on, remembering Kleissler's original point that in modernity no tradition can persist unless it becomes an object of intention held by its membership.

## The Parts of the RENEW Process

The now standard components of RENEW developed piecemeal in this experimental and open-ended way. Although parts were continually modified, the broad outline of RENEW took something like a final shape by the fall of 1978. By then RENEW was described as a process of parish renewal. Each term is significant. "Parish renewal" meant that the conversion sought would have a communal-parish reference, and "process" meant that people should not expect the final answers to religious questions that characterized pre–Vatican II Catholicism. In RENEW, laity were to be the key agents of parish conversion, another great change from pre–Vatican II Catholic life. The entire diocese was expected to adopt RENEW. RENEW was defined in communal, not individualistic, terms.

Preparing for the RENEW "process" is itself a lengthy process. The national RENEW team trains local leaders during the year preceding its implementation and the formal RENEW program lasts for two and a half years. During an overnight retreat four parishioners from each participating parish are trained to form a "core" group. They are responsible for recruiting leaders from the parish for each of the ten RENEW committees, showing again the emphasis on lay ministry. This core group then becomes the "coordinating" committee and receives more training at four diocesan-level workshops where they receive the skills and, most importantly, the confidence for their leadership in RENEW. The ten committees are:

1. Prayer network
2. Sunday liturgy committee
3. Take-home committee (prepares material for parishioners to read at home)

4. Large-group committee (sponsors one or two parish "events")
5. Small-group committee
6. "Sign-up" Sunday committee (enlists parishioners in the program)
7. Telephone committee (contacts parishioners who have not signed up)
8. Home-visit committee (visits people not reached by other committees)
9. Publicity committee
10. Evaluation committee

Each committee is provided with detailed instructions in a RENEW package published by Paulist Press. These instructions, set forth in modern management style, create the impression of a tested how-to manual, with which most middle-class people are familiar. This step-by-step methodology provides instant reassurance for any parishioner who might have doubts that she or he is good enough to be a leader in something as arcane as spiritual renewal. Local RENEW volunteers never need worry about what to do next. If God is in the details, so too is confidence for untrained laity.

RENEW comprises five six-week "seasons" that take place in the fall and during Lent (and never during Christmas or summer). Each season has a particular theme. Season 1 (fall): "The Lord's Call"; Season 2 (Lent): "Our Response to the Lord's Call"; Season 3 (fall): "Empowerment by the Spirit"; Season 4 (Lent): "Discipleship"; Season 5 (fall): "Evangelization."

## RENEW Small Groups

Although the ten committees of RENEW ensure that any parish member can participate without any taxing effort (through prayer or simply taking home some reading material), the heart of the RENEW program is the "small groups" that meet once a week during each of the five RENEW "seasons." Group facilitators receive training at a diocese-wide workshop run by the RENEW director. The RENEW manual gives this instruction:

> Ambiguity and difference of opinion should be expected and accepted. Each person should be encouraged to express his or her own feelings and thoughts, examined in light of the rich tradition of our faith. Every member of the group should experience being accepted and listened to. . . . Good moderators do not provide preambles or prologues to questions; do not frighten, shame or argue with participants by word, gesture, expression, voice tone or note-taking and do not subject the group to amateur psychiatry. A good moderator listens carefully to the participants and asks questions only when necessary to keep the discussion

moving or to keep it in focus. He or she should not know the answers to the questions beforehand, but should want to hear the group's response to the questions asked.

As mentioned earlier, RENEW emphasizes the sharing of religious feeling. Group facilitators (they are never called "leaders") are advised to encourage parishioners to "tell the story" of their lives and their faith. This emphasis on personal experience and the telling of it as a "story" is, of course, strongly egalitarian. Few of us have outstanding gifts; each of us has "experience." Everyone has a story, as bartenders know. Among the other things it does, RENEW provides everyone with a sympathetic audience.

It is probably not necessary to add that it would be naive to think that RENEW small groups achieve the kinds and depth of intensity that some claim for the "base communities" of South America. There is little sociopolitical content to the small group experience in RENEW, although the potential is there, of course. The Rev. Raymond Kemp, a speaker at the 1986 RENEW fifth annual national convention, observed that RENEW recognizes that the most elemental human need is community: "I don't know how many people I talked to who told me, RENEW helped me to make new friends. I didn't know anyone when I got here." But he immediately added the valuable observation that RENEW "declericalizes" power: "Peers are interpreting the symbols of faith for one another and that's scary. RENEW expands the number of interpreters of the meaning of being church. The RENEW goal is a community of equal ministries with a hierarchy of service."

*Linking Professionals and People*

A major aspect of RENEW's diffusion was its ability to appeal to all levels of church bureaucracy and to engage them on the local level. Modern dioceses have many different agencies and RENEW successfully enlisted their participation, a not inconsiderable achievement. RENEW's stress on process rather than substance aided this. So too did its leaders' recognition that form requires content. RENEW uses diocesan offices of peace and justice, of religious education, of liturgy, and so forth, to provide the training workshops for its large number of parish volunteers and thus has come to be seen by church professionals more as a coordinating mechanism than as a competitor.

The perception that RENEW could be used by other agencies to promote their own work was clearly a dimension of its diffusion beyond Newark. So too was its ability to appear both progressive and traditional at the same time. The enlistment of church staff gives RENEW its progressive content. But the form of RENEW ensures that professionals tailor their agendas to the local level. RENEW made sure that professional staff respect the levels of understanding of discipleship found on the local level and, since the gap between the social justice commitments found among church professionals and the average lay person is often considerable, this part of RENEW is worth some attention.

*Respecting the Ordinary: The Example of Social Justice Ministries*

The implementation of RENEW requires that diocesan offices and their staff help with the various "seasons." For example, during the preparations for Season 3 ("Empowerment by the Spirit"), local RENEW directors are encouraged to obtain the help of diocesan agencies in social justice ministries to train small-group facilitators and to plan special programs dealing with the American bishops' recent pastoral letters "The Challenge of Peace" and "Economic Justice for All." RENEW gives these staff members an opportunity to reach into local parishes that they might otherwise not as easily obtain. Here too the RENEW national staff recommends a cautious and gradual approach. But they do insist that social justice ministries and spiritual formation programs be seen as dimensions of the Christian life that require integration with parish renewal. Peace and justice staff said that RENEW had some small but worthy impacts.

Dennis Sturtevant, the director of the Catholic Human Development Office in Grand Rapids, Michigan, struck a common theme. He said that his diocese's RENEW program had resulted in a modest increase of about 10 percent in the number of parish requests for speakers, but he quickly added that "it is very difficult for the average Catholic to plug in to social justice concerns without a lot of trouble; anybody, not just Catholics." Frank Shehan, the director of the Office of Social Concerns in the Diocese of New Ulm, Minnesota, reported that the number of parishes with social concerns committees increased from three to thirty.

## RENEW as a Structure of Reconciliation

All observers of contemporary Catholicism note the great upheaval in self-understanding occasioned by the Second Vatican Council and the many contentious disputes about church life, mission, and authority that followed the council. Polls regularly show disagreements about traditional church teaching on such matters as sexual ethics and the requirements for ordained ministry. Catholicism has entered the ecumenical movement and participates in larger political and cultural debates (such as those over nuclear weapons, the economy, legal abortion), and these initiatives also involve great controversy. Catholicism has become disputatious in ways unforeseen at the time of the Second Vatican Council. A broad questioning of hierarchical authority, endemic in American life, as well as the revalorization of the role of all the baptized, ensures that the problems of pluralism and teaching authority will not be settled in any definitive or deductive fashion.

RENEW in its *form* and implementation embodies most of the themes emphasized by contemporary theology: the role of the laity, the pilgrim status of the church, the dispersion of authority in the church, the constant need for church reform, the engagement with issues of peace and justice. But the *content* of RENEW never provides an explicit position on any of these issues, although its self-description as a "process" suggests an open-endedness about future church forms. The large number of lay men and women and of women religious in RENEW programs itself exemplifies a more diffused church authority. But RENEW never explicitly raises any question about the existing modes of authority within the church or offers any explicit innovation save that of the participation of the laity promoted by the Second Vatican Council. RENEW simply requires that, in the name of local parish renewal, church conservatives, liberals, or radicals think more of communication and linkage than of ideological victory. It invites them to explore with others the root experience of being Catholic. In effect, RENEW says that all controversies are subordinated to the overriding concern of parish renewal.

Thus, RENEW contains many different kinds of appeals: mutual support in an indifferent culture; a defusing of the controversies of post-conciliar Catholicism; the need for a committed engagement in the world; the call to a universal holiness; an expansion of ministry in an era of a priest shortage; the example of the fellowship of the primitive church. These appeals, it seems to me, can connect with many different models of ecclesiology. The rationales for small groups can imply a radical critique of church, of society, or of both, as is sometimes the case for the South American "base communities." Or RENEW's promotion of small groups can simply refer to the need for emotional ties and friendship felt by many who live the dispirited individualist and competitive lives required by Western liberal capitalist culture. Most RENEW participants speak of RENEW more in this therapeutic sense (making friends, personalizing the parish, really getting to know people), but the RENEW materials can just as well be used by staff people, especially those from peace and justice offices, to carry the more demanding themes of mutual support for discipleship in a consumerist culture.

## Some Effects of RENEW

RENEW did have measurable effects, although each had to be qualified. The program worked well where the pastor promoted it, stagnated where he did not. Probably less than half of all parishes had flourishing programs, but that is a lot of parishes. The small groups, the heart of RENEW, probably attracted between 10 and 25 percent of the registered Catholics at the successful parishes. That is not a large percentage but it is a large number. If we conclude that the number of parishioners reported participating in RENEW small groups—probably less than 10 percent in larger parishes and perhaps at least 25 percent in smaller parishes —represents something less than a great impact on parish life, we should remember that even a minority, working consciously to instill a more communal spirit by greeting people, welcoming newcomers, and helping the elderly (the sorts of activities promoted in the RENEW material), can cause an alteration in atmosphere that even nonparticipants can sense. Probably as a result of RENEW, each diocese could claim several hundred disaffiliated Catholics returning to practice.

A major role of RENEW was the opportunity it provided for diocesan agencies to achieve greater coordination and gain entry in local parishes. Staff at peace and justice offices and at social concern agencies report that RENEW groups focused on charity rather than justice, but they appreciated even these small beginnings. They reported modest increases in social concern committees at the RENEW parishes. Because of their training for RENEW, parishes developed a pool of laity who felt comfortable in assuming responsibility for the wider vision of ministry required in contemporary Roman Catholicism. Parishes also reported an increased interest in the study of scripture.

In addition to these modest consequences, RENEW is also conceptually significant in that it represents an attempt to gain some breathing space from the institutional dilemmas and internal divisions that contemporary religious traditions will experience for some time. All "communities of memory" have hard times in a culture that stresses not community but individual achievement and the competitive pursuit of affluence. All traditions are constantly pressed to rethink their notions of authority and the meaning of mission.

Roman Catholicism has its own list of pressing problems concerning authority and mission, including questions about the ordination of married men and women, questions of the scope of magisterial authority, and disagreements about the ethical analysis introduced by the bishops in their pastorals "The Challenge of Peace" and "Economic Justice for All." But a continuing and contentious pluralism can be safely predicted, not only for the Catholic Christian tradition, but in all the churches. In other words, churches require "structures of reconciliation" that are not explicitly focused on reconciliation (for such a prematurity would seem to belittle the unsolved disagreements). Rather, by aiming at unarguable goods—such as RENEW's focus on parish renewal—such structures can achieve a moratorium so that the essential religious bond can be affirmed in common and with integrity. This is no easy feat, as many a parish leader has sadly discovered.

## Being Wise as a Serpent and as Innocent as a Dove: Avoiding Labels

Reflections about the success and the wide diffusion of RENEW should begin with a consideration of its pragmatic and specific origins: the preparation of parishes for mandated parish councils. RENEW's pragmatic goal stamped it with an inductive approach and its focus on the parish evoked a style of gradualism and inclusion. Although it could accommodate radical-sounding aspirations, RENEW defined itself in ways that could not be easily labeled by any organized constitutency in the Roman Catholic Church. Lacking an ideological label, RENEW never became a target. Neither liberals nor conservatives, feminists nor gender traditionalists, have opposed RENEW. RENEW never explicitly sought the conceptual breakthroughs associated with visionary thought detached from the humbling realities of local parish life. But the "moratorium" provided by RENEW should not quickly be dismissed as "regressive." For RENEW never opposed progressive reforms either, leaving both Catholic "conservatives" and "liberals" with a fuzzy target indeed. The collaborative and ad hoc development of RENEW taught its founders how to make RENEW ideologically acceptable to all parties of contention within Roman Catholicism.

RENEW became important enough to be the subject of an inquiry by the United States Bishops' Committee on Doctrine (*Origins* 16/30 [January 8, 1987]: 547–549). The report was mostly positive but expressed concern that RENEW had insufficiently emphasized Catholic identity and its doctrinal dimension. The committee also noted RENEW's lack of emphasis on the cognitive dimension of belief and its heavy emphasis on immanence with less attention to the transcendence of God, comments applicable to almost all American religiosity. RENEW staff had little difficulty in incorporating these suggestions into their written materials.

In summary, RENEW provides evidence that:

1. Ordinary church members welcome the opportunity to play formal roles in church ministry. But they must be helped to learn these roles and practice them in nonthreatening environments.

2. Small groups can deepen the fellowship of a congregation and help people learn to use scripture in their prayer life. But left unaided, small groups are likely to deepen friendships rather than discipleship.

3. Social justice and peace themes can be incorporated into a program of church renewal if professional staff are not impatient with modest achievements.

4. If ways are found to give them access to local churches, denominational professional staff need not act as nor be viewed as distant bureaucrats.

5. Traditions need ways of reasserting the primacy of the religious bond over even the successful resolution of competing definitions of church authority and of contentious issues.

6. Such a "moratorium" cannot succeed if it denies the reality and the significance of divisive disagreements within that tradition.

7. "Structures of reconciliation" probably should not directly aim at reconciliation. They should, like RENEW, aim at basic goods that require the contribution of persons who disagree even about important church questions.

Perhaps an explicitly personal note is permissible here. In a way, RENEW "solved" no church "problem." Its impacts were modest. As far as I know, the moral landscape of no city was altered in empirical ways that would invite the inquiry of skeptical sociologists. No RENEW parish advertises itself as an anticipation of the fellowship of the saints. But it was also clear that RENEW gave many thousands of ordinary people an opportunity to affirm together their tradition and the worthiness of working toward a community that prayed and served God by serving others. It emphasized ordinary lay people helping other lay people. RENEW allowed them to affirm together the core of the religious bond even in their own less than ideal parishes. More is needed; but more cannot be expected unless ordinary people can affirm the religious bond even amid contention and uncertainty. It will be decades before the many unsettling questions challenging the Roman Catholic tradition are resolved (and replaced by the next period's uncertainties). In the meantime, people need assurance that their tradition is stronger than any dispute, however serious. Many have written about the needs for renewal and for reconciliation. Few have helped us think about the *structures* that can help us to achieve both reform and reconciliation. The experience of RENEW can stimulate us to such reflections and encourage us to believe that they are possible. If we do not expect too much, much can be done.

## Some Study Questions

1. How do we try to expand the number and types of ministries in our churches?

2. Do we really believe that every last person in our congregation or parish has a role to play in its ministry?

3. What help do we provide for people to learn ministerial roles and to practice them in gradual and nonthreatening ways?

4. Do we seek ways of bringing denominational staff and its resources to help in the training of local people?

5. Do we try to integrate social justice concerns into our parish and congregational spirituality? Do we help people realize that Christian fellowship must lead to discipleship?

6. Do we acknowledge that discipleship without religious identity is most unlikely? How do we make vivid the core beliefs of our traditions? Do we believe and preach that ecumenism flourishes only where a tradition is so valued that its members eagerly seek to deepen and share that tradition?

7. Do we truly believe that our tradition is even more important than the immediate resolution of internal differences? How can we make this experience of the religious bond more real for ourselves and for our members?

8. Do those of us who think we know how to reform our churches also think about how to reconcile those who disagree with us? Do those of us who seek reconciliation in our churches also think about how we are to reform our churches?

### NOTES

For further information regarding the RENEW program, contact National Office of RENEW, George Street, Plainfield, NJ 07062. Telephone (201) 769-5400. RENEW's study guides, self-descriptions, suggested projects, and instructor's manuals are available through Paulist Press, 997 Macarthur Blvd., Mahwah, NJ 07430.

ELEVEN

# The Unfolding Story of Congregational Studies
## ALLISON STOKES AND DAVID A. ROOZEN

The essays that you have just read—or are about to read if you are one of those people who begin with the conclusion—represent much of the best current research in the field of congregational studies. Taken together they also reveal something about the complexity and direction of congregational studies as practiced today.

The essays are the work of authors whose training is in history, sociology, liturgy, hymnody, Christian education, spirituality, ecclesiology, practical theology, African-American studies, economics, political science, and so forth. They embody the most important and distinguishing characteristic of recent developments in congregational studies—namely, the realization that for any depth of praxis-oriented understanding, the local congregation must be viewed holistically from a variety of approaches. Thus scholars and consultants doing congregational studies increasingly draw upon diverse perspectives or self-consciously work in multidisciplinary teams. This was not always the case.

Just as every congregation has a particular history, which those engaged with the congregation cannot afford *not* to know (as James Lewis and James Wind tell us in their article), the field of congregational studies *itself* has a history, which it is well for those engaged with congregations to know. This may surprise many readers who are likely to be hearing of congregational studies for the first time. Do not feel remiss: it is not that you have somehow overlooked a major enterprise, but rather that this enterprise is newly coming to self-awareness.

Although the study of congregations has been an ongoing reality since the turn of the century, and in the 1920s and again in the late 1950s there were short-lived movements to systematize and expand approaches,[1] it has only been in the last decade that a named field of inquiry called "congregational studies" has emerged. With the attention of Dr. Robert Wood Lynn, senior vice-president for religion at the Lilly Endowment, grants from the endowment have stimulated a burgeoning interest and renewed focus of research in congregational studies, especially efforts to draw together fragmented approaches and learnings. With Lynn's encouragement many persons active in the study of congregations—including all the authors in this book—have been challenged to be more reflective about their practice and integrative in their perspective.

What is too easily forgotten in the midst of the current flurry of activity is that some eighty or more years ago researchers were already using the then-emerging tools of the social sciences in service of the local congregation. To the extent that there was any generic label given to the first fifty or so years of this effort, it was the "church and community census." This work was a direct response to the felt needs of congregations, denominational staff responsible for new church development, and seminary and university professors and students interested in social reform. As the American population shifted from town and country to the city, rural churches declined and urban churches sprang up. Then as new groups moved to the central cities, inner-city congregations—already at the turn of the century—were faced with the double dilemma of old constituencies moving out and new constituencies, often ethnic and poor, settling in. The need to chart and plan for demographic change—both in the declining rural areas and in the growing and the transitional urban areas—led to the earliest congregational studies.[2] These came primarily from within the old-line Protestant denominations as planners sought hard, empirical data about the numbers, kinds, and needs of people to be served.

By the end of the Depression most large Protestant church bodies had established departments of research and survey, and by the late 1950s local councils of churches in many major urban areas also had gathered together significant survey departments. In addition to their own efforts, they developed numerous guides and handbooks to assist local churches in the self-study of their community and ministry. H. Paul Douglass's *How to Study the City Church* (1928) is an early classic still well worth the reading; Mary E. Fleming's guide for cooperative religious surveys (1942) and the appendix to Murray Leiffer's *The Effective City Church* (1955) could be fruitfully read by any contemporary congregation thinking about taking a religious census of their neighborhood.

The unfolding story of congregational studies is, in fact, a story of pragmatic problem-solving. For many decades, roughly from the turn of the century through the 1960s, researchers examined the local church from *without*. They viewed its challenges in terms of the demographic changes in the social *context*, and the challenges were of two general kinds. One was the decline of establishment churches in the inner city and the development of new churches in emerging neighborhoods; the other, meeting the social and spiritual needs of the "new immigrants" to the inner-city neighborhoods being abandoned by establishment churches. The latter traces its American roots to the settlement movements of the social gospel, wherein student leaders and workers were encouraged to proceed like anthropologists in a primitive culture so that social reform could emerge out of what "the people are accomplishing for themselves both in their individual and home life, and in local organizations for whatever purpose" (Woods, 1893:68). The former began in earnest in the 1920s as the Institute for Social and Religious Research lent its support to the "church comity" movement, and it continued in fits and starts right through the mass migration to the suburbs following World War II.

Up through the 1950s researchers treated these twin challenges somewhat in tandem, and a number of studies—major in both size and significance—had already emerged by the mid-1920s. A 1922 study of Springfield, Massachusetts, for example, organized and trained a thousand church volunteers to canvass sixteen thousand households—all on a single Sunday (Douglass, 1926a). And this study was but one source for H. Paul Douglass's *1000 City Churches* (1926b), which analyzed data for 1,041 churches in fifty-six cities of all sizes across the country. As Jeffrey Hadden (1980:73–74) notes in his history of the life and work of Douglass, this book

> deserves a place as a landmark study not only for the sociology of religion, but also for the discipline of sociology. . . . Reading *1000 City Churches* more than 50 years after its initial publication does more than evoke appreciation. It provokes the mind to new and subtle ideas that have not been adequately mined.

As urban blight and suburban flight quickened in the 1960s, the emphasis in contextual studies swung decidedly toward the prophetic, and works like *The Noise of Solemn Assemblies* (Berger, 1961), *The Suburban Captivity of the Churches* (Winter, 1961), and *The Comfortable Pew* (Berton, 1965) replaced the affirmative realism of church development studies with a critical idealism that wedded theological and social analysis. Even such an otherwise descriptive and insightful study as Metz's *New Congregations* (1967) concludes by arguing that the growth mentality of new churches produces a self-centeredness and need for security that makes it difficult for these congregations to turn to social service and justice-oriented ministries once they are firmly established. One ironic twist in the prophetic turn in congregational studies was that as social justice issues came to dominate the ethos of ecumenical Protestantism, the large denominational research departments built up through the 1950s were severely cut back, and those located in local councils of churches totally dismantled. As a result, the published literature in congregational studies became and remained for many years the exclusive domain of academics.

Following the 1960s and parallel to the broader cultural turn from social idealism to self-fulfillment/realization/actualization in the early 1970s, contextual studies of the congregation gave way to examining the local church from *within*. "Renewal" became the new metaphor, and researchers began to view a congregation's challenges as issues of internal *process* and *program*. It was a time, as the title of James Anderson's book announced, *To Come Alive!* (1973), and congregational studies focused on planning, conflict, leadership, stewardship, and a host of other organizational dilemmas perhaps best exemplified in the twenty-five titles in the Creative Leadership series edited by Lyle Schaller and published by Abingdon Press, beginning in the mid-1970s. Even the American Church Growth movement—with its creative and symbolic center at Fuller Seminary, and by far the most prolific single source of congregational studies since the demise of the Institute for Social and Religious Research in the early 1930s—looked to a congregation's internal dynamics as the key to evangelistic success.

Issues of context, process, and program continue to draw the attention of both churches and researchers. But today, as congregations struggle with problems of *identity* in a world increasingly secular and pluralistic, a more holistic research approach is beginning to emerge, as the essays in this volume suggest. It is in many ways a response to the challenge of the multiplicity of social and religious forces that erode a congregation's unity of vision, and it is an affirmation that a congregation's inherited and confessed, formal and informal, web of symbolic meaning, values, and commitments—that is, its culture—always consciously or unconsciously informs pragmatic choices made among the diverse alternatives of program, process, and context with which every congregation is continually confronted.

In order to comprehend congregational studies as it has evolved, is currently practiced, and is likely to take shape in the future, one must take into account the role of the social sciences. The establishment of congregational studies was contingent upon the coming into being of the disciplines of sociology and anthropology, in particular. It simply never occurred to anyone to rigorously examine the local congregation in its concrete particularity until social scientific methods were applied to analyzing human and organizational behavior. Reciprocally and somewhat ironically, the originating impulse for the development of sociology in America was the applied concern for social reform stimulated by the social gospel movement.[3]

For the first half of this century practitioners of congregational studies were predominantly sociologists. With the emergence of the social science subspecialty known as organizational development (OD), and the turn in emphasis within congregational studies from focusing on context to focusing on process and program beginning in earnest in the 1970s, OD (or "process") consultants became increasingly prominent among congregational study practitioners. Today, with increasing concern about congregational identity and culture, anthropological and sociohistorical approaches and insights are being added to the mix.

Is it important for leaders of congregations—whether ordained or lay— to know these things, to be familiar with the unfolding story of congregational studies? Does having some knowledge of the field make a difference? We suggest that it does, for four important reasons.

First, the disciplined understanding of the dynamics of a congregation increases one's capacity to be faithful and effective within it. The findings of congregational studies practitioners point to a richness, depth, and complexity to congregations seldom before imagined, appreciated, or described. They also point to the uniqueness of individual congregations, which defy translation between congregations and which demand an appreciation for the concrete particularity of each. As Denham Grierson (1984:16) notes in making the case for particularity, three propositions about any congregation are true:

> Each congregation is like every other congregation. Some congregations are like some other congregations. No congregation is like any other congregation.

He then proceeds to argue that while the first two receive the majority of attention in the theological literature, the latter is foundational to transforming a people of God.

A second reason for knowing something about congregational studies, a corollary to the first, is that faithful and effective ministry grows out of the tension between vision and reality; and in the theological world, as every pastor entering her or his first pastorate quickly learns, there is a decided tendency to slight the concrete and often bulking reality of actual congregations for the vision of gospel imperatives. Oliver Whitley's *The Church: Mirror or Window?* (1969) provides ample illustration. For example, then-contemporary definitions of the church and the dominant trends in ethical thinking were based on the assumption that a congregation was, in a meaningful sense, a primary group and a reference group, whereas the weight of empirical research on congregations indicated that, at least in mainline congregations, this assumption was not generally true. Congregational studies can be a helpful corrective toward reestablishing the tension, and to use Grierson's (1984:39) evocative phrase, of identifying "openings for ministry" that can serve as the basis for creative ventures toward greater faithfulness.

A third reason for entering the world of congregational studies is that here congregations will find a deep reservoir of useful resources for discovering and articulating the "openings for ministry" of which Grierson speaks; for naming and transcending those frustrating blocks to change that we all experience; and for (in the words of the contributors to the *Handbook for Congregational Studies*; Carroll, Dudley, and McKinney, 1986:7) taking "seriously and appreciatively, through disciplined understanding, their present *being*—the good and precious qualities that are within them—as means of grace themselves that enable the transformation of congregations into what it is possible for them to *become*."

The essays in this volume, as well as the *Handbook for Congregational Studies*, Grierson's *Transforming a People of God* (1984), and Abingdon Press's Creative Leadership series noted above, are excellent, recent, and somewhat diverse starting points for those interested in mining the resources available in the field of congregational studies. But they are only the tip of the iceberg. Some time ago when the authors of this article began to assemble a comprehensive bibliography of books and articles in congregational studies for our own edification, we found more than seven hundred published items, a few dating from just before the turn of the century. The best published bibliography to date, Carl Dudley and James Hopewell's "Understanding and Activating Congregations," appears in *Building Effective Ministry* (Dudley, 1983:246–256). The authors of this bibliography provide much guidance and help by dividing the books into three general categories—missional studies, studies of church functions, and descriptive research—and then into many subcategories—administration of the congregation, congregational renewal, conflict management, and the like. The endnotes to chapter 2 in Hopewell's provocative *Congregations: Stories and Structures* (1987:30–39) also constitute a rich bibliographic overview. They reemphasize that the unfolding story of congregational studies is primarily a story of pragmatic problem-solving.

A final reason for knowing something about the field of congregational studies is to gain insight into where the future is leading us. In its earliest days the study of the local congregation was founded and promoted by white, reform-minded Protestant sociologists like H. Paul Douglass. Today blacks as well as whites, Roman Catholics and Jews as well as Protestants, evangelicals as well as liberals, and scholars from the humanities and the classical theological disciplines as well as behavioral scientists are turning to the disciplined and appreciative study of the congregation. Moreover, not only academics and religious professionals but also lay people in congregations are increasingly taking an interest in the transformation of their congregations and the helpfulness of disciplined study toward this end. Open to constant innovation and responsive to changing research methods, the field of congregational studies has been expanding and evolving for nearly a hundred years, the latest tack being toward cross-disciplinary approaches that recognize that it is the whole that gives meaning to the parts, rather than the parts to the whole.

But what has *rarely* happened and needs to happen is a sharing across ethnic and faith boundaries. While studies of the congregation have helped us to understand how congregations are carriers of tradition, the enterprise has been rather tightly circumscribed within the traditions themselves. Because there is little dialogue across the lines that divide us, our learning is necessarily limited and there is a built-in conservatism in uncritically accepting the perspectives of any particular subculture. The congregational history project represented in chapter 1 of this volume and the church and community project represented in chapter 6 are therefore especially noteworthy in their efforts to cross ethnic and faith boundaries.

It is a truism that one knows oneself through encounter with the other; that one best recognizes one's unique particularity in dialogue with the universal. So it is with congregations in their rich pluralism. Congregational studies today is full of ferment and promise. In the future we can hope for more of the kind of high-level meeting, dialogue, and exchange to which this volume in its inclusion of black and white, Protestant and Roman Catholic traditions begins to point.

## NOTES

1. The two most significant efforts to systematize and expand congregational studies prior to the 1980s were those of (1) the Institute for Social and Religious Research, and (2) the National Council of Churches' Bureau of Research and Survey, especially its late 1950s effort to study "the effective city church." Under the leadership of such pioneering figures as H. Paul Douglass, C. Luther Fry, and Edmund de S. Brunner, the Institute for Social and Religious Research published seventy-eight volumes from its inception in 1921 to its demise in 1934. It is viewed by many as not only the center of religious research during this period, but also the leading center for nonacademic sociology (Hadden, 1980). The National Council of Churches' effective city church study was initiated at the very zenith of denominational research, shortly after a major consultation to address "the shortage of personnel to answer the mounting planning and research needs of the church" (Bureau of Research and Survey, 1960:1). Unfortunately both the consultation and the launching of the effective city church study fell victim to the changing denominational priorities of the 1960s and never realized their promise. In fact, Kloetzli's *The City Church* (1961) was the only vestige of the effective city church study to find its way into print.

2. While the urban situation has received the majority of attention in congregational studies, there is a significant literature on the rural church stretching from at least Gill and Pinchot's *The Country Church* (1911) and Boisen's "Factors Which Have Contributed to the Decline of the Country Church" (1916) to Hassinger, Holik, and Benson's *The Rural Church: Learning from Three Decades of Change* (1988).

3. See, for example, Vidich and Lyman's *American Sociology: Worldly Rejections of Religion and Their Directions* (1985).

## WORKS CITED

Anderson, James
    1973     *To Come Alive! A New Proposal for Revitalizing the Local Church.* New York: Harper & Row.

Berger, Peter
    1961     *The Noise of Solemn Assemblies: Christian Commitment and the Religious Establishment in America.* Garden City, N.Y.: Doubleday & Co.

Berton, Pierre
    1965     *The Comfortable Pew: A Critical Look at Christianity and the Religious Establishment in the New Age.* Philadelphia: J. B. Lippincott Co.

Boisen, Anton T.
    1916     "Factors Which Have Contributed to the Decline of the Country Church." *American Journal of Sociology* 22 (September): 177–193.

Bureau of Research and Survey, National Council of Churches
 1960  "Consultation on Church Planning and Research." *Information Service*, May 28, pp. 1–8.

Carroll, Jackson W., Carl S. Dudley, and William McKinney, eds.
 1986  *Handbook for Congregational Studies*. Nashville: Abingdon Press.

Douglass, H. Paul
 1926a  *The Springfield Church Survey*. New York: George H. Doran Co.
 1926b  *1000 City Churches*. New York: George H. Doran Co.
 1928  *How to Study the City Church*. Garden City, N.Y.: George H. Doran Co.

Dudley, Carl S., ed.
 1983  *Building Effective Ministry: Theory and Practice in the Local Church*. San Francisco: Harper & Row.

Fleming, Mary Eldon
 1942  "A Study of Needed Guidance for Cooperative Religious Surveys." M.A. thesis, Presbyterian College of Christian Education, Chicago, Ill.

Gill, Charles Otis, and Gifford Pinchot
 1911  *The Country Church: Decline, Influence, and Remedy*. New York: Macmillan Co.

Grierson, Denham
 1984  *Transforming a People of God*. Melbourne: Joint Board of Christian Education of Australia and New Zealand.

Hadden, Jeffrey K.
 1980  "H. Paul Douglass: His Perspective and His Work." *Review of Religious Research* 22 (September): 66–88.

Hassinger, Edward W., John S. Holik, and J. Kenneth Benson
 1988  *The Rural Church: Learning from Three Decades of Change*. Nashville: Abingdon Press.

Hopewell, James F.
 1987  *Congregation: Stories and Structures*. Edited by Barbara G. Wheeler. Philadelphia: Fortress Press.

Kloetzli, Walter
 1961  *The City Church—Death or Renewal: A Study of Eight Urban Lutheran Churches*. Philadelphia: Muhlenberg Press.

Leiffer, Murray
 1955  *The Effective City Church*. New York: Abingdon Press.

Metz, Donald L.
 1967  *New Congregations: Security and Mission in Conflict*. Philadelphia: Westminster Press.

Vidich, Arthur J., and Stanford M. Lyman
    1985       *American Sociology: Worldly Rejections of Religion and Their Directions.* New Haven, Conn.: Yale University Press.

Whitley, Oliver Read
    1969       *The Church: Mirror or Window? Images of the Church in American Society.* St. Louis: Bethany Press.

Winter, Gibson
    1961       *The Suburban Captivity of the Churches.* Garden City, N.Y.: Doubleday & Co.

Woods, Robert A.
    1893       "The University Settlement Idea." In *Philanthropy and Social Process: Seven Essays Delivered Before the School of Applied Ethics at Plymouth, Mass. During the Session of 1892.* New York: Thomas Y. Crowell.